CHESS *for absolute beginners*

International Grandmaster

RAYMOND KEENE

Artistic Consultant

BARRY MARTIN

B.T. Batsford Ltd, *London*

First published 1993
© Raymond Keene 1993
All illustrations except chess diagrams
© Barry Martin 1993

ISBN 0 7134 7208 1

British Library Cataloguing-in-Publication Data.
A catalogue record for this book is available
from the British Library.

Typeset by Lasertext Ltd, Thomas Street,
Stretford, Manchester M32 0JT
and printed in Hong Kong

for the publishers,
B.T. Batsford Ltd,
4 Fitzhardinge Street,
London W1H 0AH

To Alexander and Jessica

A BATSFORD CHESS BOOK
Adviser: R. D. Keene GM, OBE
Technical Editor: Andrew Kinsman

Contents

ACKNOWLEDGMENTS

The author would like to gratefully acknowledge the following people for their assistance in the preparation of this book: Annette Keene and Annette Hardman for typing; Tony Buzan for advice on educational presentation; Andrew Kinsman for editorial work; and Peter Kemmis Betty for his support of this project. Finally, my thanks to Barry Martin, who trained at University of London Goldsmiths' College and St Martin's School of Art, for his unstinting assistance and artistic inspiration.

Raymond Keene
March 1993

Introduction to Chess

WHAT IS CHESS?

CHESS is a mind game played between two opposing sides — Black and White. The object of the game is to kill the opposing king — to give checkmate.

CHESS is a microcosm of battle, with forces, led by the king, symbolically based on the military units of the Indian Army of 300 BC when the game was probably invented.

CHESS is the world's most gripping mental sport. It has fascinated men and women, artists, philosophers, writers and players for around two thousand years. Chess was mentioned by Shakespeare, Goethe, Leibnitz, Benjamin Franklin and Einstein. Tsar Ivan the Terrible, Elizabeth I, Catherine the Great and Indira Gandhi have all played chess, or owned stunningly beautiful chess sets.

CHESS grandmasters now compete for prizes in excess of $5 million.

CHESS is played regularly by millions of people around the world, both to relax and to stimulate their minds. The champions of chess, players such as Paul Morphy, Emanuel Lasker, José Capablanca, Alexander Alekhine, Bobby Fischer, Gary Kasparov, the fabulous Polgar sisters and Nigel Short are venerated as heroes by their followers.

CHESS is a game with no physical, sex or age barriers. A girl of eight will often be seen beating grown men!

CHESS has a vast literature, preserving the very best of its achievements stretching back two millennia!!

'CHESS is fun and you make a lot of new friends out of it. There are lots of small rules in the competitions but it's rather easy to learn the basic moves.'

Luke McShane (World Under-Ten Champion and the youngest chess master in history)

THE FASCINATING HISTORY OF CHESS

The modern form of chess, with the sweeping power of queens and bishops and the ability to castle, became popular in the 1470s, although it was not until the mid-eighteenth century that the first recognised master of the modern game emerged, André Philidor. Chess as we know it evolved from an ancient game called shatranj which had been popular for many centuries.

Shatranj — The Old Arabic Form of Chess

Although traditional sources give the date for the origination of chess as around AD 500, I believe that we must place it much earlier, since already by the eighth and ninth centuries AD the Baghdad Caliphate could boast several players whose relative strength in shatranj was equivalent to that of Philidor's at the modern game. Shatranj theory was widely published in manuscripts, some of which survive to the present day. Is it conceivable that such a rich chess culture, with such expertise, could have existed in Baghdad at that time if chess had only existed for two centuries? I believe that we must search back earlier, indeed as far as 350 BC, for the roots of shatranj, the Muslim game, and ultimately of modern chess.

Shatranj

An early Arabic form of chess in which the queen and bishop were restricted in comparison to their modern counterparts. Although this Muslim game was slower than modern chess, it was still recognisably chess and was very popular in Baghdad by the eighth century.

The Impact of Alexander the Great

Aristotle, the tutor of Alexander the Great, mentions in his *Politics* a group of classical Greek games which were collectively known as petteia. These were games of a battle type which demanded skill, logic and pure reason, not just the fortune associated with a throw of the dice. These games are also mentioned by Plato in *The Republic*, where he compares Socrates's victims, who are finally trapped and made helpless by didactic, to 'Weak petteia players, who are finally cornered and rendered unable to move by stronger ones'. Around 330 BC Alexander the Great invaded Persia and marched on towards Asia Minor and India. En route he founded Hellenic colonies in which the Greeks, assuming that they were good students of Plato and Aristotle, would have played petteia.

Chess as a Reflection of the Old Indian Army

At this time chaturanga, a battle game using dice, was played in India. Its sanskrit name, meaning 'four divisions', was also used for the Indian army, consisting of elephants, chariots, cavalry and infantry. The word 'chaturanga' may look alien, but becomes at once more familiar if one compares it to the French word for four, 'quatre' or the Russian 'chitiri'.

The Greek and Indian Fusion

In the centuries following the establishment of the Hellenic colonies chaturanga, the Indian war game of chance, met petteia, the Greek game of reason. The effect of petteia on chaturanga was to eliminate the dice element and throw the players on their own resources of the mind. From this collision of cultures chess, Greek thought expressed in Indian language, was born.

The Power of the Queen

It was not until the late fifteenth century that the surprisingly swift transformation, through which chess emerged from the chrysalis of its slow Islamic form, began. It was then that castling was introduced, pawns gained the privilege of advancing two squares on their first move, and the queen switched from being a waddling cripple (the Arabic vizier) to the most power-fully mobile piece on the board. Doubtless the almost overnight increase in the strength of the queen explains why many of the early recorded games with the new chess show the queen in joyous adventures, often giving check regardless of whether this furthered the player's cause or not.

The Renaissance Dynamic

Chess is a game which symbolises warfare, so the increased fire power of the queen surely reflects the introduction of battle-field artillery in the mid-fifteenth century. The sudden advances in chess as a whole must also be explicable in terms of the Renaissance dynamic; the increasingly urgent perception of distance, space and perspective which distinguished that phase of human intellectual development. The innovatory use of siege artillery to batter down the walls of Constantinople in 1453, scientific developments such as the tele-scope and the microscope, and the use of perspective in art were all parallel develop-ments.

Columbus and the Spanish Legacy

The third country which had a decisive influence on the spread of chess, apart from Greece and India, was Spain. Columbus discovered the New World for Spain in 1492 and it is fitting that the impetus for the newly developed form of chess should also have come from Spain. Chess spread rapidly after 1475 because Spain was the dominant centre for world communication and Spain spread the new chess globally through her explorations and conquests. The Spanish conquistadors were, in fact, well known for playing chess and teaching it to the conquered Inca and Aztec kings.

On his return Columbus presented his discovery of the New World to Ferdinand and Isabella of Spain at the Salon Noble Tinell, the very building in which Gary Kasparov won the Barcelona leg of the chess World Cup in 1989. In 1519 Magellan set off on the first circumnavigation of the planet from the Guadalquivir river in Seville. Seville was also the venue for the 1987 Kasparov-Karpov match, the first all-Soviet World Championship match to be held in is entirety outside the Soviet Union. These events underline the Spanish chess legacy.

The Spanish Opening

Spain even has its own chess opening — the Ruy Lopez, or Spanish Opening, as it is known on the continent. This was invented by Ruy Lopez, the sixteenth-century Spanish priest and native of Estremadura, and the leading player of his age. Lopez's chess skill made him a favourite at the court of King Phillip II and also something of an international celebrity. In 1560 Lopez visited Rome on ecclesiastical business and defeated the best Italian players. On his return to Spain in 1561 Lopez published his own chess book, entitled *Libro de la Invencion Liberal y Arte del Juego de Axedrez* which contained general advice and some recommended openings. The Ruy Lopez is still one of the major highways of chess opening theory and is a particular favourite of World Chess Champions Bobby Fischer and Gary Kasparov, and also of Britain's World Championship Challenger, Nigel Short.

The Limitlessness of Chess

Computer programmers believe that they will be able to devise a program which can beat Gary Kasparov, but only when their machines can calculate at the astronomical rate of 1 billion (1,000,000,000) moves per second. This speed of calculation is not yet technically feasible, even for a modern super-computer.

An Arabic legend relates the story of the doubling of squares to show the astounding numbers associated with chess. The legend goes that the inventor of chess, when asked to name his reward by a grateful monarch, asked merely for a quantity of grain — one grain of corn for the first square on the chessboard, two for the second, four for the third and so on, doubling each time. The emperor readily agreed, only to discover to his stupefaction that the final quantity was unimaginably large. The number of grains on the last square would be 2^{63} and the total $2^{64} - 1$. This comes to around 18,000,000,000,000,000,000 grains of corn, payment of which would be enough to bank-rupt several empires!

A grandmaster game is classed as a 'mini-ature' if it lasts only 25 moves or less. If one decided to print out every possible game of chess of this nature, in books the size of, and with the same typeface as, the London telephone directories, you would have to cover the surface of the earth totally and then work outwards, filling all available space, to a distance in every direction equal to that from earth to the farthest known galaxy, not once but 10^{20} times, that is, 10 followed by 19 zeros.

Chess and the Human Brain

But I have saved the best and most mind-blowing statistic till last. The numerology of chess may be vast, but consider this — in your brain there are a minimum of a million million (1,000,000,000,000) neurons or brain cells. Each of these neurons can simultaneously interact with from 1 to 100,000 other neurons in a diverse number of ways. The number of possible connec-tions, of thought-maps, in your brain dwarfs even the colossal number of possible games of chess. In fact, the pattern-making capa-city of your brain is so great that it would take a line of figures of more than 10.5 million kilometres in length simply to write it out. The brain, your brain, is limitless.

So — chess may be endlessly fascinating and endlessly mysterious, but it is also, for your human brain, easy to play and to play well!

This book tells you how to start on this enjoyable and stimulating path, one which will enrich and reward you for the rest of your life.

GOALS OF THE GAME

From your point of view, there are three possible results to any game of chess:

1) You win;
2) You lose;
3) The game ends in a draw.

You win when you deliver checkmate or when your opponent realises the hopelessness of his or her situation and resigns.

You lose when this scenario is reversed.

The game can end in a draw at any stage by mutual agreement. Stalemate, when one side physically cannot move, is also a draw. A draw can also come about if the position has become sterile and there can clearly be no decisive result, i.e. when there are just lone kings on the board, when the position has been repeated three times with the same player to move, or when fifty moves have been played without a piece being taken or a pawn moved.

The Starting Position

'We play the game of war imitating the real thing.'

MARCUS HIERONYMOUS VIDA,
Bishop of Alba and Cremona,
De Ludo Scaccorum,
1513

Chess is a mind game, representing a battle, played by two opponents, each having an army of sixteen pieces on a chequered board of 64 alternate light and dark squares. At the start of the game, each player's pieces are arranged in rows along the first two ranks, with a light square in the bottom right side of the board. The infantry, the pawns, occupy the front rank and behind them stand the more important pieces. In the centre of this row lies the king, whose capture or 'checkmate' terminates the game, and next to the king the queen, the strongest piece on the board. Then come, in feudal hierarchy, the bishops, the knights and finally the more powerful rooks (or castles).

Black is always at the top

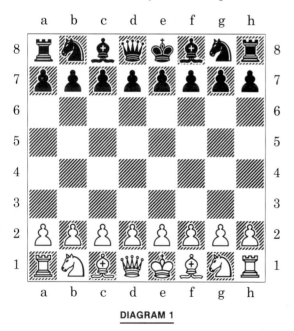

DIAGRAM 1

White is always at the bottom

The ultimate object of the game is to trap (checkmate) the opposing king, so that it has no hiding place. If a player gives checkmate then he or she has won the game. If there is no checkmate the game can end in a draw. Certain positions are technically drawn (for example, when only the two opposing kings are left on the board) while a draw can also be agreed by the two players at any time, if they so wish.

At the start of the game White moves first, then Black, and each side continues to make alternate moves. A player may not miss a turn. If he or she is unable to make a legal move the game will have ended, either in checkmate, or in a draw by stalemate. These terms will soon be explained in greater detail.

After the initial moves, the two armies move into combat. Enemy pieces can be removed from the board (captured) by occupying their square with one of your own pieces. There are three main phases to the game: the opening; the middlegame; and the endgame. At all stages two golden rules should be borne in mind.

1) Watch out for snap checkmates, either for you or against you;
2) Always capture your opponent's pieces if it is safe to do so, and make sure that you spot threats to your pieces by the opponent!

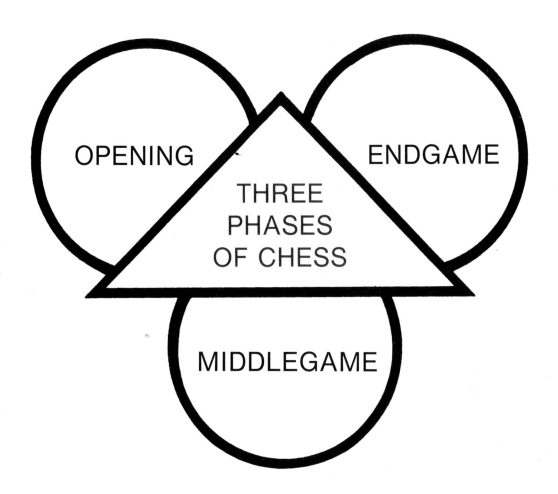

How to Read the Moves

The Board

The moves in this book are given in the universally recognised and employed 'algebraic notation'. This describes a very simple way of writing down the moves. You must be able to follow it in order to understand the information in this book.

Look at **Diagram 2**. The co-ordinates running round the edge of the chessboard determine the designation of every single square on the board. Each square is described by a letter (referring to the columns or 'files' which run from the bottom to the top of the board) followed by a number, which refers to the 'ranks' running across the board.

Thus, in **Diagram 2**, the square marked with an X is e4. This system will immediately be familiar to everyone who has ever used a road map or an A–Z street guide. The principle is exactly the same. Every diagram in this book will be furnished with these co-ordinates to help you follow the moves.

Piece Moves

To read or record a move by a piece; first of all, the move number is given, e.g. 1, 2, 3, 4 or 5 etc. Then comes the name of the piece (K, Q, R, N or B). Next comes the square on which the piece started. Finally, the square to which it travels. Thus in **Diagram 3**, it is clear that White plays 1 Ng1–f3.

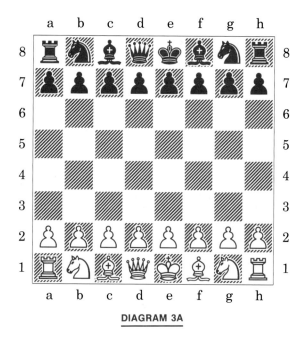

DIAGRAM 3A

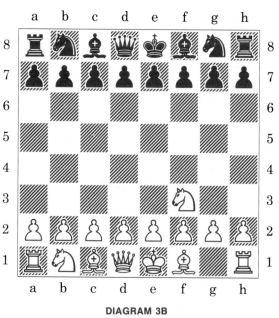

DIAGRAM 3B

DIAGRAM 2

Pawn Moves

Pawn moves follow exactly the same principle, with the exception that we do not bother to preface the pawn move with a P. Therefore, 1 d2–d4 means that on the first move, White moves the d-pawn from d2 to d4.

Captures

Captures also follow exactly the same principle except that the capture is indicated by an 'x'. Thus after the moves 1 e2–e4 e7–e5 2 Ng1–f3 Ng8–f6 White can now play the capture 3 Nf3xe5. **Diagram 5** shows the position before and after this capture has taken place.

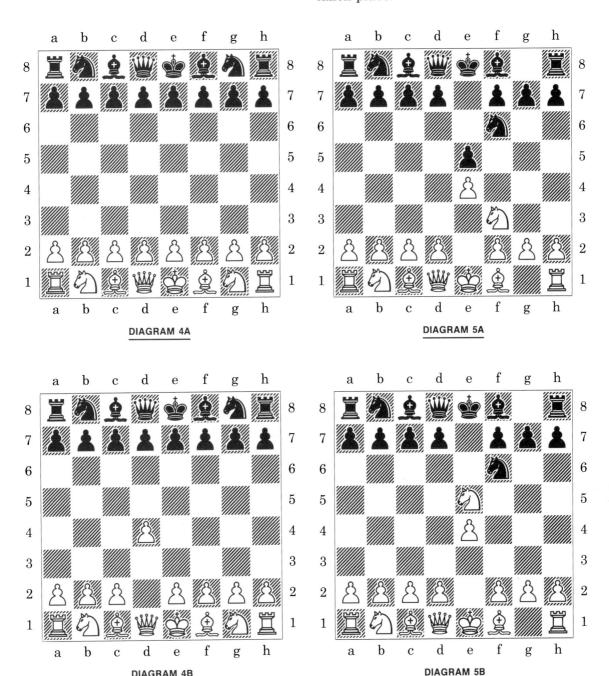

DIAGRAM 4A

DIAGRAM 5A

DIAGRAM 4B

DIAGRAM 5B

The Pieces

How to Capture

It is a basic rule of chess that two pieces cannot occupy the same square simultaneously: when a unit moves to a square already occupied by an enemy piece a capture takes place, and the original resident is killed i.e. taken from the board. The capture of a unit belonging to one's own side is not permitted. In contrast to draughts (checkers) there is no obligation to capture, unless that is the only way to counter a threat to your king.

There is, however, a basic obligation to move; passing or missing a turn is not allowed in chess. If the side whose turn it is to move is not in check and has no legal moves, this is called *stalemate* and the game immediately and automatically terminates in a draw.

The Pieces

Over the next few pages the reader will be introduced to the various pieces, discovering the powers and limitations of each. At the end of the section the reader will find a series of exercises, most of them fairly simple although one or two are quite complex. Primarily they are there to provide practice and increased comprehension, but many have considerable intrinsic interest. This is because either they illustrate situations which are quite often reached in actual play or because they show in miniature form important tactical or strategic ideas. The reader is urged not to skip these little problems, but to try and solve each one as you come to it. The solutions will be found at the end of the section (page 36).

THE VALUES OF THE PIECES

It is vitally important to realise and remember that most chess games are decided by extra material! Either through your own good play, or through your opponent's carelessness (or vice-versa), one player will obtain a material advantage sufficient to determine the outcome of the game. Even at beginner's level the loss of a piece without compensation usually results in the loss of the game; in master games the loss of even a single pawn can be equally disastrous.

Not all chess pieces have equal value: a queen is worth more than a rook; rooks are usually stronger than bishops and knights; and so on. It is natural to ask if we can be more precise than this: can we quantify the relative strengths of the pieces? This question is of practical as well as academic interest because frequently in game situations you will be faced with the possibility of exchanging some combination of your own forces for a different selection of your opponent's pieces. You will then have to decide whether such an exchange favours you or not.

Here is a 'point-count' table to help you estimate the relative strengths of the pieces.

Symbol	
P	Pawn = 1 point
N	Knight = 3 points
B	Bishop = 3 points
R	Rook = 5 points
Q	Queen = 9 points

So, if you capture three pawns in exchange for a knight, you still have approximate material balance. The same would be true if you had a rook and one pawn against bishop and knight. However, if you take your opponent's queen and only lose a rook for it, you would certainly be doing very well!

Needless to say, the table gives no value for the king since this piece can never be exchanged (if you like the king is worth an infinite number of points).

This simple point-count table must be committed to memory! It will form the basis for many of your most important decisions on the chessboard.

Figurine Algebraic Notation

In magazines and books, including this one, pieces are usually represented by a 'figurine' rather than by an abbreviation.

N = ♘
B = ♗
R = ♖
Q = ♕
K = ♔

THE KING

The Most Important Piece

The prime directive of chess is to surround the enemy king, i.e. to deliver checkmate. This is what makes chess so special. But the king's move itself is simple: one square in any direction.

There is one exceptional case, called castling, in which the king moves two squares in one turn. Castling is a combination move of two pieces at once, so we shall postpone discussion of this case until we know something about the rook, which is also involved in the castling operation. For the moment, we shall concentrate on a few important points.

The king is highly manoeuvrable but is not a long-range piece — its sphere of influence is confined to the adjacent squares. To attack enemy units it must move up next to them and if caught in an advanced position it can retreat only relatively slowly. These factors combine to limit the usefulness of the king as an aggressive force; king safety must always be paramount (remember, the object of the game for each player is to checkmate the enemy king!).

Mobilise Your King in the Endgame

Generally speaking, it is only in the later stages of the game (the ending), when most of the pieces have been exchanged off through captures and the chance of a snap checkmate is diminished, that the king emerges as a fighter; earlier on, especially when the queens are on the board, the risk of exposure is too great and the king's role tends to be defensive in character.

The King on the Edge of the Board

The activity of the king — measured by the number of possible moves it can make, or equivalently, by the number of squares it controls — is diminished if it is placed on the edge of the board. We shall see this exploited repeatedly in elementary mating situations (king and queen against king, for instance) where the first stage in delivering the mate is to force the king to the edge where its freedom of action is vastly reduced.

DIAGRAM 6A

The diagram shows the moves of the white king. From e4 the king can reach any of the squares marked with an arrow.

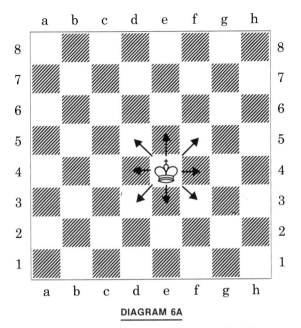

DIAGRAM 7A

In this diagram, with White to move, his king can capture the black rook.

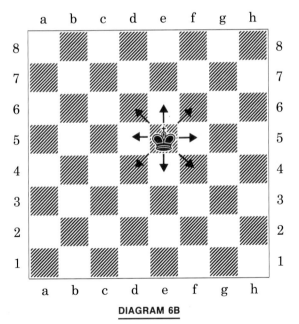

DIAGRAM 6B

This diagram shows the moves of Black's king from e5. From that square it can move to any of d4, e4, f4, d5, f5, d6, e6 and f6.

DIAGRAM 7B

White to move here as well. Once again, the king can take the rook.

THE QUEEN

The king may be the most important piece on the chessboard but the queen is the most powerful. The queen moves along any number of empty squares along a rank, file or diagonal in a single move. She cannot turn corners, nor move through or on to a square already occupied by a friendly unit. The queen cannot move through a square occupied by an enemy piece, although she can move on to such a square, capturing the hostile unit on that square, In common with the bishop, the queen can never jump over any piece, whether it is yours or your opponent's.

Diagram 8 shows a queen on an otherwise open board. In one move the queen can reach any one of the squares indicated along the arrows in the diagram, a staggering total of 27 possible moves. No wonder the queen is so powerful!

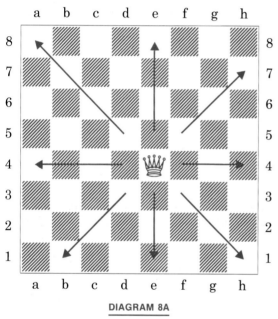

DIAGRAM 8A

The arrows indicate the enormous range of a centrally placed queen. Her Majesty may travel to any square along the arrowed lines, an amazing range of choice.

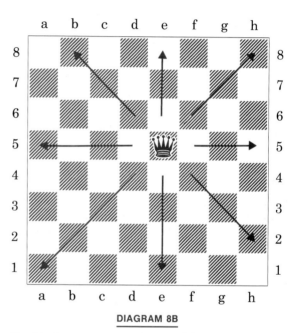

DIAGRAM 8B

The black queen can go to any of these squares in this diagram: a5, a1, b2, b5, b8, c3, c5, c7, d4, d5, d6, e1, e2, e3, e4, e6, e7, e8, f4, f5, f6, g3, g5, g7 and h2, h5, h8. A grand total of 27 squares!

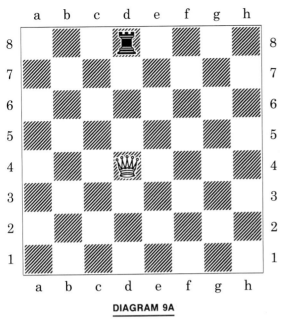

DIAGRAM 9A

The white queen, with White to move, may take the black rook.

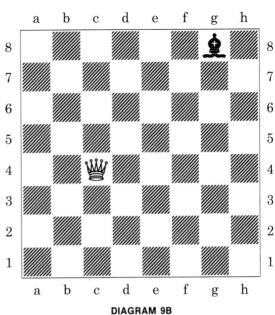

DIAGRAM 9B

White to move. The white queen can take the black bishop.

Whatever you do, try not to lose or exchange your queen for anything less than checkmate or the capture of your opponent's queen. The player who wins the queen tends to win the game as well, so take extra care at all times not to place your queen in danger.

The queen gained her immense powers of mobility in the late fifteenth century. The transformation from the older weaker piece known as the vizier or minister, was perhaps a sort of homage to the powerful ruler, Queen Isabella of Spain, the patron of Christopher Columbus.

WIN THE QUEEN!
WIN THE GAME!!

THE ROOK

Rooks move only along ranks and files — never along diagonals. In one move a rook can travel as many squares as it likes along a rank or file, provided that there is nothing blocking its path. As with the queen, a rook cannot move through a square occupied by another unit. The rook captures in the usual way — by moving onto the square of the man it captures. The rook's action is illustrated in the following diagram.

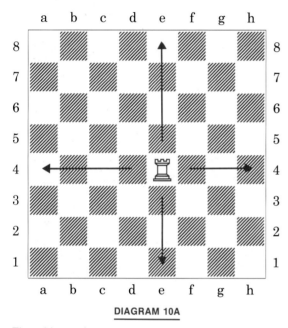

DIAGRAM 10A

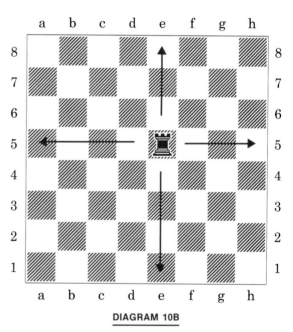

DIAGRAM 10B

The white rook may move to any square along the arrowed lines. The lines going across are ranks and those going vertically are files.

The black rook can also move to any square on the arrows, a5, b5, c5, d5, e1, e2, e3, e4, e6, e7, e8, f5, g5 and h5, fourteen in all.

Where to Put Your Rooks

In **Diagram 11A** the rook can reach any square marked along the arrows in a single move. Notice that, unlike the other pieces, a rook's activity is not necessarily reduced if it is positioned at, or near, the edge of the board — it still controls the same number of squares. In most positions the critical factor determining whether or not a rook is actively placed is the presence (or absence) of open lines along which the rook can operate. Nevertheless, it is usually good advice to move your rooks towards the centre when you are mobilising your pieces. It is a common error to leave the rooks languishing in the corner on their original squares, while the main battle is raging in the centre of the board.

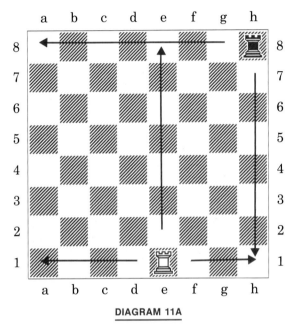

DIAGRAM 11A

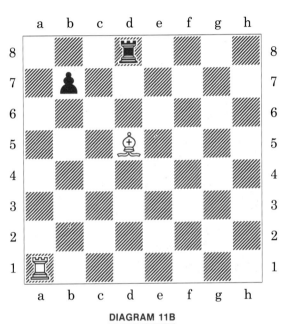

DIAGRAM 11B

Interestingly, the black rook and the white rook can both reach fourteen squares, even though one is in the centre and the other on the edge.

Rook captures: Black to play can take by ... ♖xd5. White to play cannot take ♖xb7. The pawn is on the wrong file to be captured.

Rook or Castle?

The rook looks like a castle. Indeed, young players will often call it a 'castle', and why not? In French, German, Spanish and Italian, the rook is quite correctly referred to as the 'tower' or the 'castle'. Use of the term 'rook' in chess probably comes from the ancient Persian word 'rukh' for war chariot or, perhaps, from 'rocco', an Italian alternative for tower.

THE BISHOP

Each side has two bishops, one operating exclusively on light squares and the other on dark squares. The bishops sweep along the chessboard on the diagonals, and the two diagrams show the territory which can be covered by a bishop.

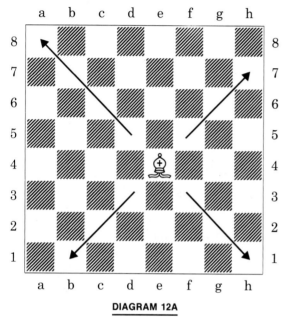

DIAGRAM 12A

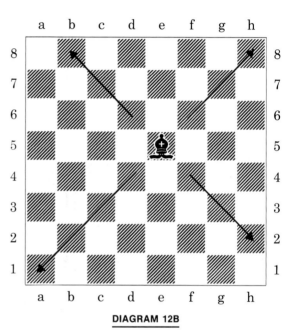

DIAGRAM 12B

The arrows indicate the field of action of the white bishop. Note that this piece must always stay on the light-squared diagonals, but in the centre of the board this still leaves a choice of thirteen squares to which the bishop can move.

Black's bishop can go anywhere along the marked arrows, a1, b2, b8, c3, c7, d4, d6, f4, f6, g3, g7, h2, and h8. The dark-squared bishop must remain permanently on dark squares, never straying to the light ones.

The bishop (along with the knight), is regarded as a 'minor' piece, the 'major' pieces being the rook and the queen. The bishop is worth the equivalent of a knight or of three pawns in terms of playing power.

If the bishop's path is unrestricted by any other piece, then it can move to any square along its diagonal route. It cannot, though, leap over pieces in its path, but it can capture an opposing piece that is in its way by landing on and occupying that piece's square.

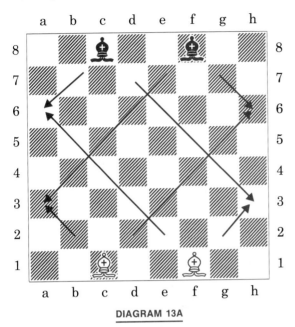

DIAGRAM 13A

All four bishops are seen on their starting squares. The arrows indicate their field of activity.

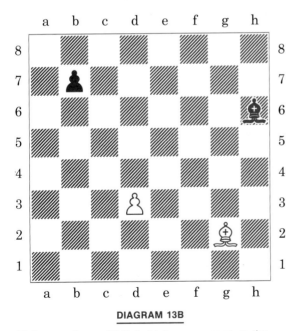

DIAGRAM 13B

Bishop captures: White's bishop can capture the black pawn on b7. Black's bishop cannot take White's pawn on d3.

From Pachyderm to Prelate

Chess reached its first great flowering in northern India at the end of the sixth century AD. The piece we now know as the bishop has a colourful history. It was then represented as an elephant, one of the four branches of the Indian army, along with the infantry (pawns), the cavalry (knights) and the chariots (now depicted as rooks or castles). The elephant can still be found today on ornate chess sets made in India and other Asian countries; the Russian word for bishop is 'Slon', meaning Elephant!

As chess spread from India to other cultures, the pieces were modified to reflect the societies that it penetrated. Chess reached Europe by the end of the tenth century and here the elephant was not a familiar sight. So the piece appeared in a variety of alternative guises.

The famous Isle of Lewis pieces dating from the twelfth century do, in fact, include bishops. The Lewis chess pieces (now in the British Museum) are probably Viking in origin, but other societies depicted the same piece in a variety of ways. In Germany the bishop is known as a runner or messenger; in France as a fool, or court jester. In the first book printed in English *Game and Playe of the Chesse* (1474), William Caxton suggested that the piece should be represented by a judge, sitting in a chair with an open book. Despite Caxton's suggestion, it is as a bishop that the piece is best known today in the English-speaking world.

The Knight

The move of the knight is a fabulous leap over any intervening obstacle. This is probably best illustrated by a diagram: White's knight can reach any one of the eight squares indicated by an 'x' in **Diagram 14A**.

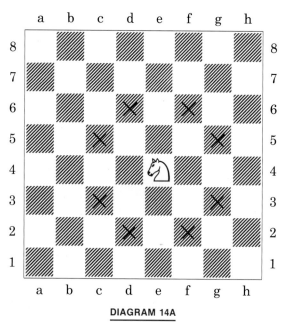

DIAGRAM 14A

The white knight can leap to any square marked with a cross.

Diagram 14B shows that the knight can also reach the same squares even if it is totally surrounded by other pieces, be they friendly or hostile ones. Over friend or foe alike, the knight can still make its jump and knights capture in exactly the same way as they move.

Near the edge of the board the knight has less mobility. For example, a knight on a1 can reach only the squares b3 or c2 in one move. So you can see that knights are much better positioned in the centre of the board than on the edge.

The knight is always represented by a horse. Because of its unusual move, a sudden knight attack can often cause havoc in the enemy camp!

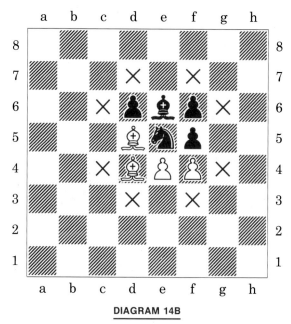

DIAGRAM 14B

The black knight can also jump to any of the marked squares: d7, c6, c4, d3, f3, g4, g6 and f7, eight in total. Even surrounded by pieces or pawns, whether hostile or friendly, the knight can still jump to the marked squares!

The Knight Raid

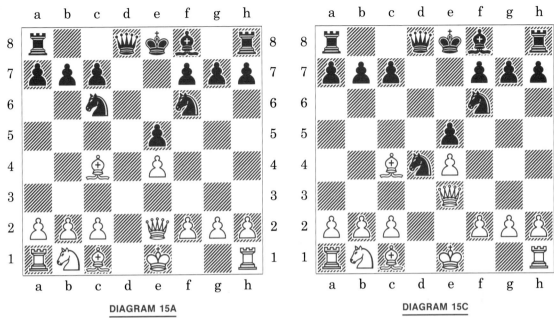

DIAGRAM 15A

Black to move is poised to invade White's position with his knight on d4.

DIAGRAM 15C

White saves his queen from attack, but this is a poor square, as we shall see.

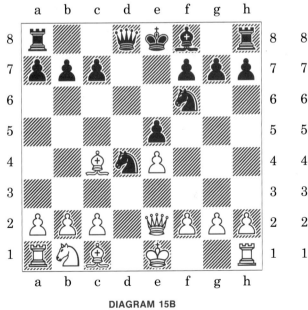

DIAGRAM 15B

Black's knight jumps into the centre with a typical attack against White's queen. White cannot capture the knight, so he must make a decision about where to place the queen.

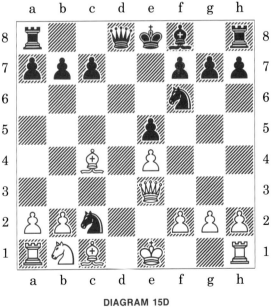

DIAGRAM 15D

Black's knight takes on c2, with a devastating triple attack against White's rook (a1), queen (e3) and king (e1). This typical attack is known as a knight 'fork'.

THE PAWNS – THE FOOTSOLDIERS OF CHESS

'Every soldier carries a marshal's baton in his knapsack.'

NAPOLEON

For most of the game the pawn's role is to secure and hold down territory or perhaps to expend itself in an assault against the enemy positions.

But the chess player's army is a meritocracy: one does not have to be born into the officer caste. Any pawn which survives long enough and advances far enough will suddenly find that it has been transformed into that most glorious of pieces — the queen.

Philidor's Rule About Pawns

The eighteenth-century master André Philidor said of pawns that they were the 'soul of chess'. They add a much needed strategic element to what would otherwise be an almost purely tactical game. Piece configurations are fluid and can change rapidly. In contrast, pawn formations are relatively static and often remain stable for extended periods. You can build your whole game around them. Indeed, many more grandmaster chess games are won through exploiting weaknesses in the enemy pawn structure than through direct attacks against the opposing king.

How Pawns Move

Now we need to look at how the pawns actually move. The most basic characteristic of pawns is that, like the grenadiers in the army of Frederick the Great, they travel in only one direction — forwards. When moving to an empty square pawns normally move one square at a time along the file. An exception is made if the pawn has not previously moved and is still on its starting position; then it may, for its initial move only, advance two squares along the file instead of one (it is not obliged to move two squares — this is only an extra option). Pawns have a quite different action when capturing: they capture by moving one square forward diagonally. They cannot capture straight ahead. The various types of pawn move are illustrated in **Diagrams 16 and 17**.

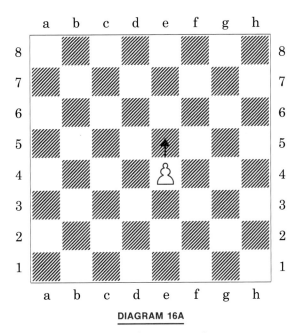

DIAGRAM 16A

The white pawn can only move to e5.

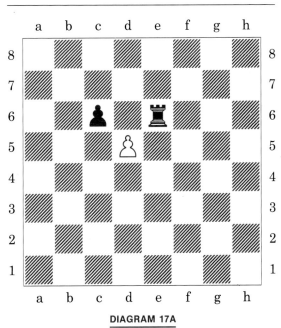

DIAGRAM 17A

Pawn captures: White to move can play either d5xc6 or d5xe6. Black to move can take: . . . c6xd5.

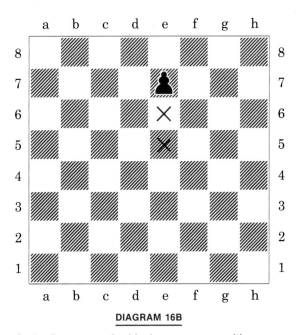

DIAGRAM 16B

On its first move, the black e-pawn may either go to e6 or e5.

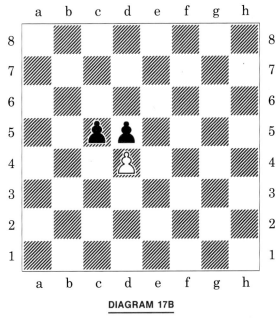

DIAGRAM 17B

White to move can take: d4xc5. Black to move can take: . . . c5xd4.

Pawn Promotion

As the game progresses, the pawns will move further down the board away from their home squares. When a pawn reaches the eighth rank — the opponent's back rank of the board — it has gone as far as it can go and runs out of normal moves. A transformation then takes place and the player who owns that pawn must replace it by any other type of piece of his colour that he desires (except a king). This process is called *promotion* or, more popularly, *queening a pawn*, since in actual play one almost always chooses to promote to a queen. Subsequently, the promoted pawn behaves exactly as if it were an ordinary queen or whichever piece was chosen. Amazingly, it is theoretically possible for a player to have as many as nine queens on the board at one time. There is no restriction on the number of pawns which a player can promote. However, the pawn is the only piece which promotes upon reaching the eighth rank — only the private soldier has the marshal's baton.

But remember — Pawns Can Never Retreat!

Other uses for Pawns

Pawn promotion usually occurs in the later stages of the game when the position has become simplified. In the opening and middlegame it is much more difficult to clear a path for the advancement of a pawn. However, pawns have many uses apart from the ability to promote: in the early stages of a game their function is to secure and hold territory, to deny the use of key squares to your opponent, and to support your own pieces in advanced positions. Furthermore, one group of pawns will usually be assigned the task of forming a defensive barrier in front of your own king to ensure the monarch's safety.

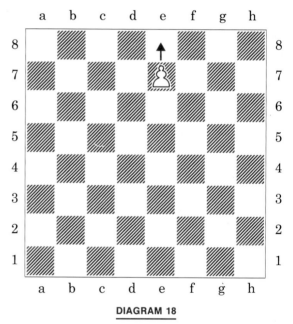

DIAGRAM 18

The white pawn can advance to e8 and become a queen. One normally promotes to a queen, since this is by far the most powerful piece.

The Passed Pawn – A Potential Queen

A pawn is called 'a passed pawn' when no hostile pawn can impede its path towards becoming a queen. A passed pawn is often a considerable advantage because of the constant queening threats which it generates, simply by advancing. For a pawn to be truly 'passed', there must be no enemy pawn in front of it, either on the pawn's own file or on either of the files adjacent to the passed pawn. Thus, if White has a pawn on the e-file, for it to qualify as a passed pawn there must be no black pawns ahead of it on the d-file, the e-file or the f-file. **Diagram 19** should make this quite clear.

It is good to create your own passed pawn, especially if it can be securely protected by another of your pawns. A supported passed pawn is a real asset, but even better is two passed pawns, side by side, which often constitute a deadly force. They can advance in unison, chasing your opponent's pieces out of their path. On the other hand, keep a very close eye on possible advances by any of your opponent's passed pawns!

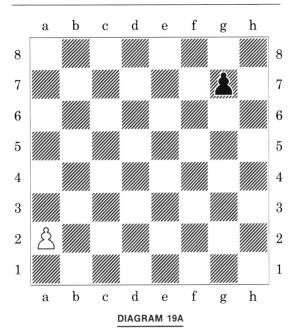

DIAGRAM 19A

The black g7-pawn is passed. So is the white pawn on a2.

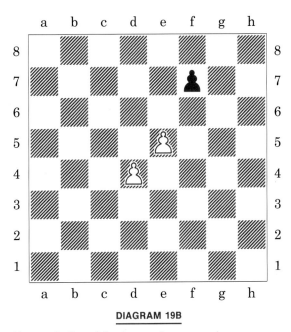

DIAGRAM 19B

Here only the white d-pawn is a passed pawn.

A Special Case — The En Passant Pawn Capture

There is one other special situation involving pawns which we have not yet described — the en passant capture. The possibility of an en passant capture (referred to as 'e.p.'), arises only when a pawn on its starting square takes advantage of its initial move of two squares forward. Now an enemy pawn which could have captured it if it had moved only one square forward still has the same opportunity! This special rule allows the opponent on his next move only to play the pawn capture as if the pawn had only moved one square forward. **Diagram 20** illustrates what happens when the possibility of an en passant capture arises.

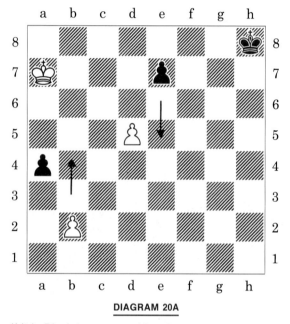

DIAGRAM 20A

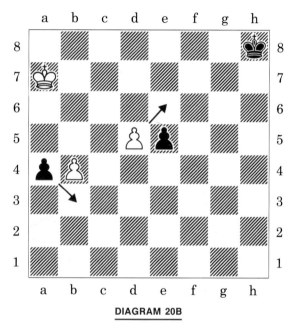

DIAGRAM 20B

If it is Black to move and he plays ... e7–e5, White may take d5xe6ep. If White moves b2–b4, Black may take by a4xb3ep.

It is important to remember that the option to capture en passant must be exercised immediately, as soon as your next moves comes, or not at all.

The en passant rule is not as arbitrary as it might at first sight appear. In earlier days, before the rules of chess had been completely codified, pawns were only allowed to move one square forward at a time in all positions. The initial double-square pawn move was introduced to speed up the game, but this innovation had one deleterious side-effect: it became possible to use the double move to block a pawn position. So the en passant rule was invented to prevent this from happening — keeping positions open, fluid and ready for dashing attacks.

Is En Passant Worth Remembering?
Yes, definitely! En passant will not happen very often in your games, but you must be aware of the possibility. Who knows, you may catch out an opponent who doesn't know the rule, and thereby win an important pawn!

By the way, en passant means, as you would expect, 'in passing'.

Here is an easy to remember summary of what we have learnt about pawns:

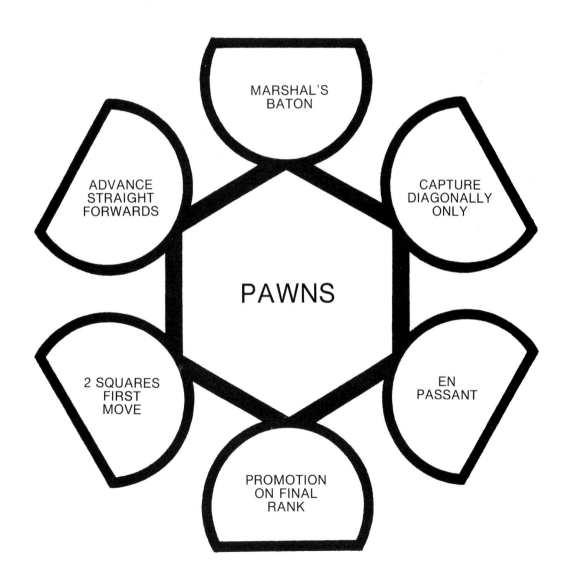

MARSHAL'S BATON

ADVANCE STRAIGHT FORWARDS

CAPTURE DIAGONALLY ONLY

2 SQUARES FIRST MOVE

PAWNS

EN PASSANT

PROMOTION ON FINAL RANK

PUZZLES

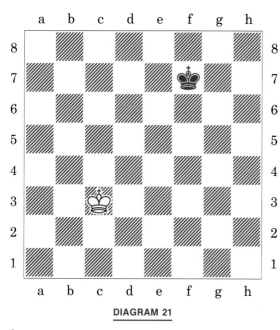

DIAGRAM 21

1
A) List all the squares White's king can reach in one move.
B) Can Black play ... ♚f7–d6?

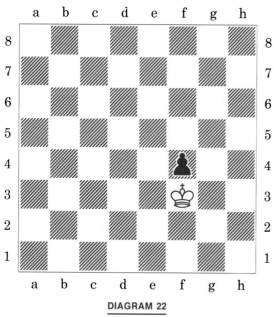

DIAGRAM 22

2
A) Is White's king in check?
B) Can White's king capture the pawn?

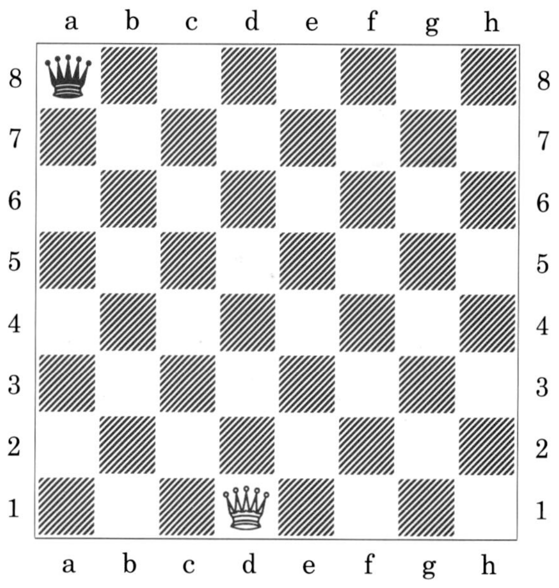

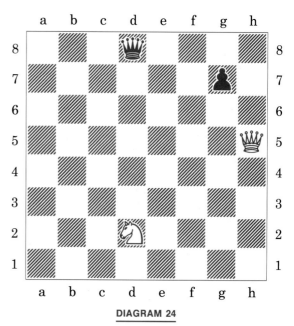

DIAGRAM 23

3
A) Can White's queen take Black's queen?
B) Can Black play ... ♛a8–g2?

DIAGRAM 24

4
A) Can Black take by ... ♛d8xd2?
B) Can White take by ♛h5xg7?

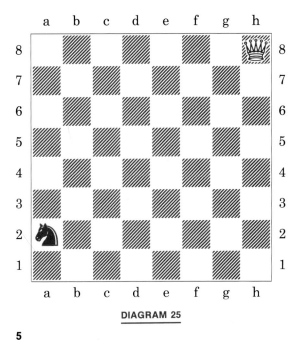

DIAGRAM 25

5

A) Can White's queen take Black's knight?

B) Can Black's knight go to c1?

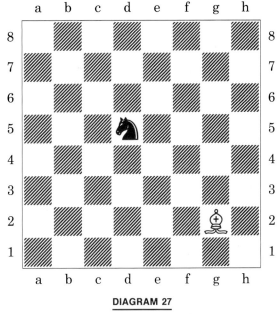

DIAGRAM 27

7

A) Can White play ♗g2xd5?

B) Can Black play ... ♘d5–b3?

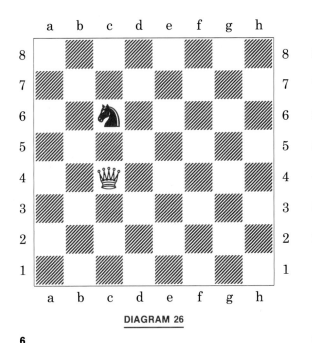

DIAGRAM 26

6

A) Can Black's knight take White's queen?

B) Can White play ♕c4–c5?

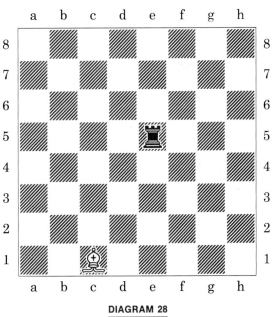

DIAGRAM 28

8

A) Can White's bishop take Black's rook?

B) Can Black play ... ♖e5–d5?

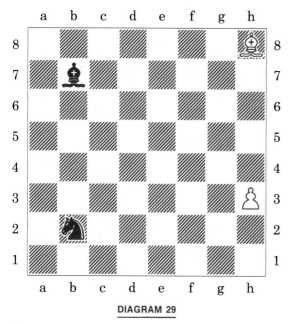

DIAGRAM 29

9

A) Can White's bishop take Black's knight?

B) Can Black's bishop take White's pawn?

C) Can Black play ... ♝b7–h2?

D) Can White play h3–h5?

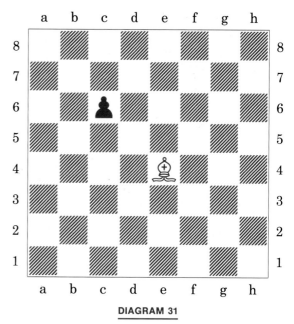

DIAGRAM 31

11

A) Can White play ♝e4xc6?

B) Can Black play ... c6–d5?

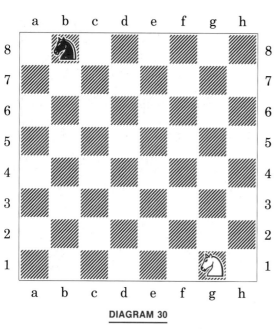

DIAGRAM 30

10

A) List all legal moves by White's knight.

B) Can Black play ... ♞b8–b6?

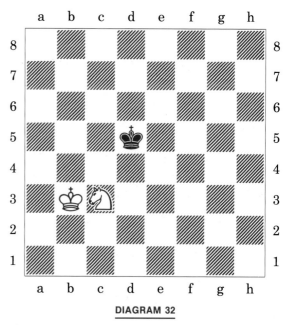

DIAGRAM 32

12

A) Is Black in check?

B) List all of Black's legal moves.

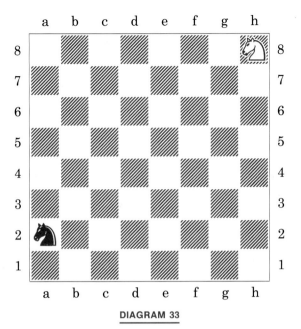

DIAGRAM 33

13
A) List all of White's legal moves.
B) List all of Black's legal moves.

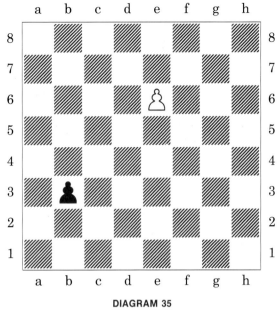

DIAGRAM 35

15
A) Name any passed pawns.
B) White to play — who promotes first and to what?

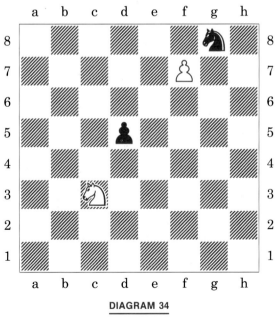

DIAGRAM 34

14
A) How many ways can White promote his pawn to a queen?
B) Can White take ♘c3xd5?

DIAGRAM 36

16
A) List White's possible moves.
B) List Black's possible moves.

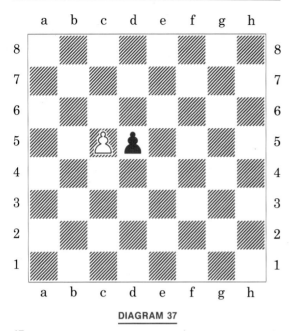

DIAGRAM 37

17

Black has just played ... d6–d5. Can White take en passant?

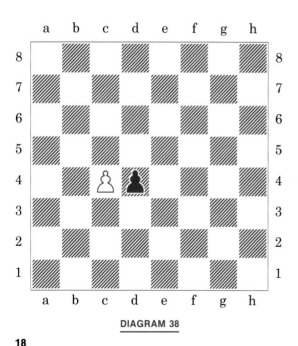

DIAGRAM 38

18

White has just played c2–c4. Can Black take en passant?

ANSWERS

Here are the answers to the puzzles you have just tackled. You should be able to score 100% if you have understood the book so far. If you managed this proceed to the next chapter. If not, keep a note of which questions have foxed you, and go back to look at the relevant explanatory sections again before proceeding.

1
A) White's king can move to b4, c4, d4, b3, d3, b2, c2 and d2.
B) Black cannot play ... ♔f7–d6. Kings do not jump except in castling.

2
A) White's king is not in check.
B) White's king can capture the pawn.

3
A) White's queen cannot take Black's queen.
B) Black can play ... ♕a8–g2.

4
A) Black can take by ... ♕d8xd2.
B) The move ♕h5xg7 is not legal and cannot be played.

5
A) No, White's queen cannot take Black's knight.
B) Yes, Black's knight can go to c1.

6
A) Black's knight cannot take White's queen.
B) Yes, White's queen can go to c5.

7
A) Yes, ♗g2xd5 is possible.
B) Black cannot play ... ♘d5–b3.

8

A) White's bishop is not attacking the black rook and, therefore, cannot take it.

B) Yes, Black can play ... ♖e5–d5.

9

A) Yes, ♗h8xb2 is possible.

B) No, ... ♗b7xh3 is not legal.

C) No, ... ♗b7–h2 is impossible.

D) No, h3–h5 is not legal. Pawns can only move two squares at once on their first turn.

10

A) ♘g1–h3, ♘g1–f3 and ♘g1–e2 are all the legal moves of White's knight.

B) No, Black cannot play ... ♘b8–b6.

11

A) White can play ♗e4xc6.

B) Black cannot play ... c6–d5. Pawns only move diagonally when making a capture.

12

A) Yes, Black is in check.

B) Black's legal moves are to play his king to any of the following squares: c6, d6, e6, c5, e5 and d4. The square e4 is attacked by White's knight and is, therefore, not accessible to the black king. The square c4 is also covered by a white piece, the king.

13

A) White can play ♘h8–f7 or ♘h8–g6.

B) Black can play ... ♘a2–b4, ... ♘a2–c3 or ... ♘a2–c1.

14

A) White has two ways to promote his pawn to a queen, either f7–f8=♕ or f7xg8=♕.

B) Yes, White can play ♘c3xd5.

15

A) The white pawn on e6 is passed and so is the black pawn on b3.

B) If it is White to play, he plays 1 e6–e7. Black plays ... b3–b2. White now plays 2 e7–e8 and promotes first. The pawn can become either a queen, rook, bishop or knight. However, one should, as a rule, promote to a queen since this is the most powerful piece.

16

A) White's possible moves are: a7–a8=♕, a7–a8=♖, a7–a8=♗ or a7–a8=♘.

B) Black's possible moves are: ... d2–d1=♕, ... d2–d1=♖, ... d2–d1=♗ or ... d2–d1=♘.

17

No, White cannot take en passant. You can only capture en passant when a pawn moves from its starting square.

18

Yes, Black can play ... d4xc3 en passant since White's pawn moved from its starting square.

Special Rules

CASTLING

There is a special move involving the king and either of your rooks called castling. Castling is extremely important; it represents the symbolic entry of the king into its fortress. It is also a vital method of moving your rook quickly to the centre, where it is most useful. I strongly urge you to castle early in all your games. If you castle your king quickly escapes from the centre, where it is at its most vulnerable. Conversely, if your opponent delays castling, you may be able to mow down his king while it is still on its home square!

How Castling Works

Depending on whether the king's rook or the queen's rook is used we speak of castling kingside or castling queenside. Castling is the only move in which two of your own pieces change position simultaneously and there are strict rules which determine whether you can castle or not. The most basic requirements to be met before castling can be carried out are that neither the king nor the rook involved may have made any previous moves (so both will be on their starting positions), and that the squares between the king and rook must be vacant. The castling manoeuvre consists of moving the king two squares along the back rank towards the rook and then moving the rook to the square through which the king has just passed. Thus, in **Diagram 39** we see White before and after having castled kingside: the king moves from e1 to g1 and the king's rook from h1 to f1.

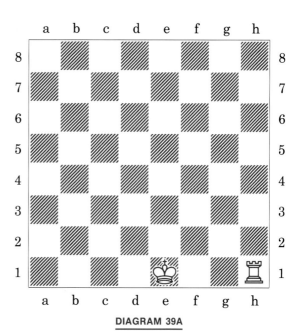

DIAGRAM 39A

Before castling kingside for White.

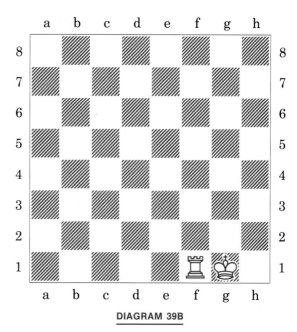

DIAGRAM 39B

After castling kingside for White.

The analogous move with the queen's rook, queenside castling, is shown in **Diagram 40**: Black's king moves from e8 to c8 and his rook moves from a8 to d8.

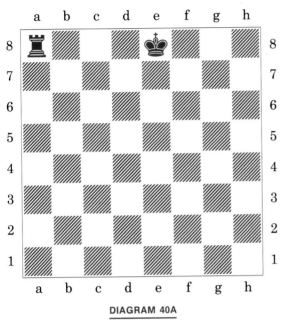

DIAGRAM 40A

Before castling queenside for Black.

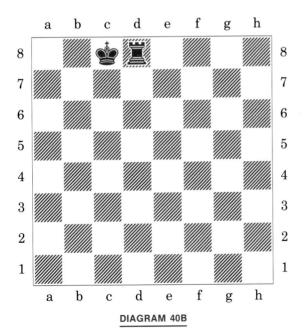

DIAGRAM 40B

After castling queenside for Black.

These are two further conditions which must be satisfied before castling is possible:
1) The king may not castle if it is in check — but once the check has been removed it retains the right to castle later, provided that it has not moved in the meantime. Of course, the king may not castle into check either.
2) Castling is prohibited if the square through which the king passes (i.e. the square on which the rook finishes) is under attack by an enemy unit.

It is possible to castle even if the rook involved is threatened. Also, queenside castling *is* permitted even if the square b1 (or b8 in Black's case) is under fire, since this square is not one through which the king crosses.

Remember:

Kingside castling for both White and Black is written down as 0–0, whilst queenside castling for both sides is written down as 0–0–0.

Finally, when castling it is a convention in chess to touch and move the king first.

Castling in practice

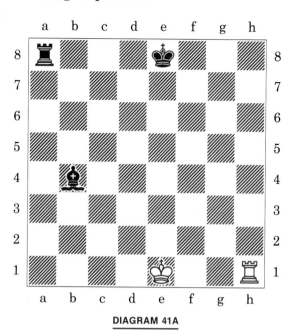

DIAGRAM 41A

CASTLING NOT LEGAL FOR WHITE
White is in check from the black bishop on b4. You cannot castle out of check! (Of course Black cannot castle because White is in check so it must be his move.)

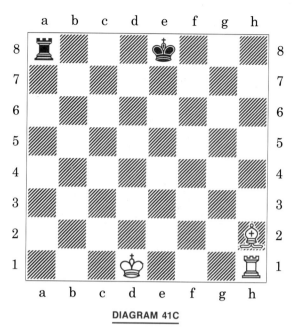

DIAGRAM 41C

CASTLING NOT LEGAL FOR WHITE BUT LEGAL FOR BLACK
White cannot castle because his king has moved from its starting square. Black can castle. It is irrelevant that White's bishop controls b8, since the black king does not pass over that square.

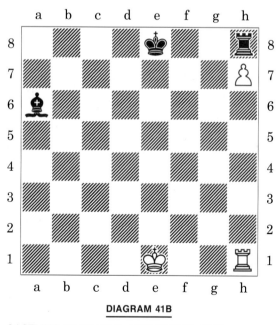

DIAGRAM 41B

CASTLING NOT LEGAL FOR EITHER SIDE
White cannot castle, since the black bishop attacks f1. Black cannot castle since White's pawn attacks g8.

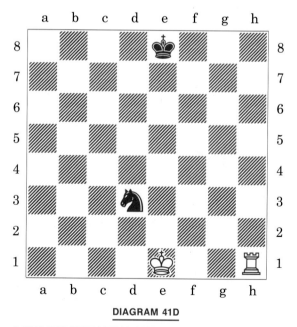

DIAGRAM 41D

CASTLING NOT LEGAL FOR WHITE
White cannot castle, since he is in check from the black knight. After moving his king out of check he will never be able to castle.

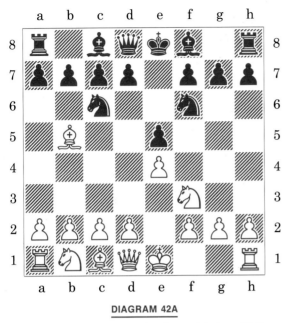

DIAGRAM 42A

A standard opening (the Ruy Lopez) before White castles kingside.

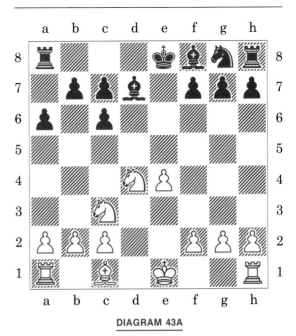

DIAGRAM 43A

Another typical opening before Black castles queenside.

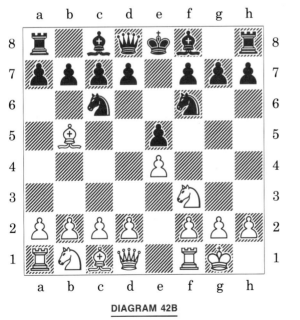

DIAGRAM 42B

After White castles kingside.

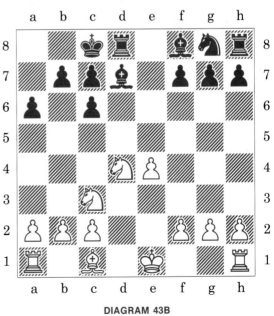

DIAGRAM 43B

After Black castles queenside.

WHAT IS CHECK?

We have discovered how all the pieces move and now it is time for you to understand the concept of check from a piece to the king, how it is given and how it is parried.

The King in Check
The giving of check underlines the special nature of the king in chess. A king is said to be in check when it is threatened with capture by an opposing unit. A player whose king is in check has as his or her sole duty to avert the danger to the monarch, i.e. to get out of check immediately. If this is impossible then checkmate has occurred and the game is over. Royal suicide is prohibited — it is illegal to leave or put one's own king in check.

How to Parry a Check
There are three ways of evading a check:
1) By moving the king out of harm's way;
2) By capturing the enemy man which delivers the check; or
3) (If the king is being attacked from a distance.) By interposing a friendly unit to block the check. Of course it is impossible to interpose in the case of a knight check. If more than one way of stopping a check is possible, then you must choose whichever move is best.

Announcing Check
If a player is in check and plays a move which fails to stop the check, then this move is illegal and must be retracted. To alert the opponent and avoid embarrassment some players courteously announce the fact that they have played a checking move by saying 'check' as they make the move. This practice is less common among masters, who are expected to notice such things for themselves. It is, however, customary to indicate a check when writing down a move; this is done by adding the symbol '+' at the end of the ordinary description of the move. Thus, the difference

between moves written down as ♕d1–h5 and ♕d1–h5+ is that the latter attacks the enemy king while the former does not.

The king is what makes chess so extraordinarily different from other board games, such as Go, Draughts or Backgammon. In these games all the pieces have the same initial value — loss of one particular piece does not signify immediate loss of the game — but in chess it does!

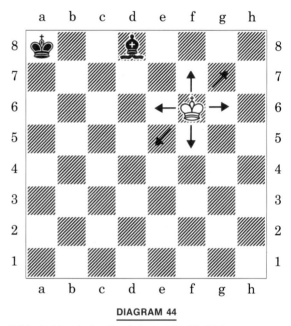

DIAGRAM 44

White's king is in check from Black's bishop and must move. The arrows indicate which squares are legal refuges.

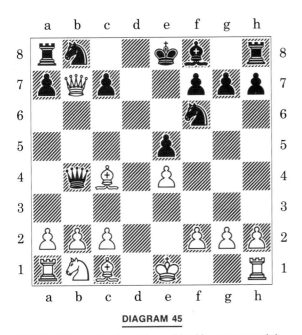

DIAGRAM 45

White's king is in check from Black's queen on b4. Let us examine the three ways of stopping the check:

1) White can move his king with ♔e1–f1 or ♔e1–e2 or ♔e1–d1.

2) White can take the black queen with ♕b7xb4.

3) White can interpose a piece to block the check. There are four moves to achieve this, namely, c2–c3, ♘b1–c3, ♘b1–d2 and ♗c1–d2.

Of all these choices, White's only good move is choice 2, ♕b7xb4.

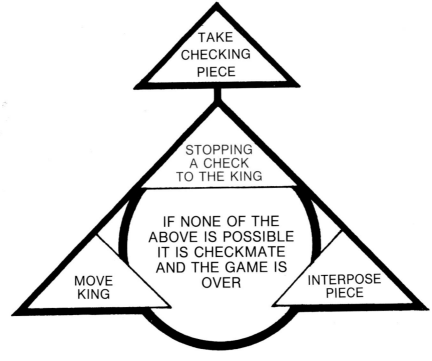

WHAT IS CHECKMATE?

Now that you understand how all the pieces work, I will give some examples of possible checkmate positions.

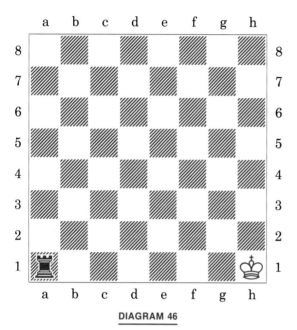

DIAGRAM 46

This is check. You know it well. White can escape with his king moving to g2 or h2.

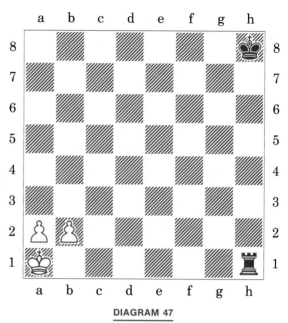

DIAGRAM 47

But this is more serious — White is in check from the black rook, and there is no escape route. It is checkmate! White's pawns trap his own king.

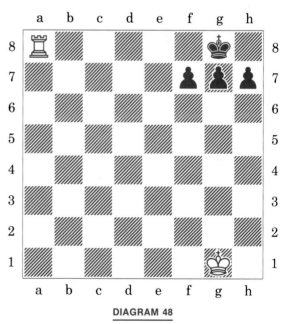

DIAGRAM 48

Another example of checkmate by a rook on the back rank. This is one of the most common types of checkmate, so always keep an eye out for it if your king, or your opponent's, does not have a bolthole in the pawns around it.

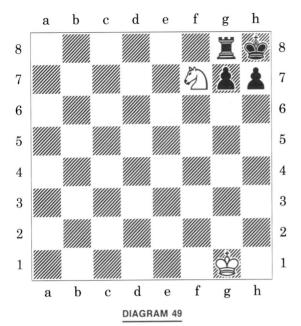

DIAGRAM 49

A dramatic 'smothered mate' with the knight imprisoning Black's king.

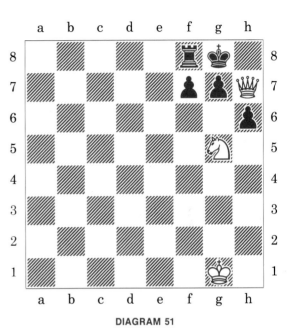

DIAGRAM 51

A very typical checkmating motif with the white queen playing the main role.

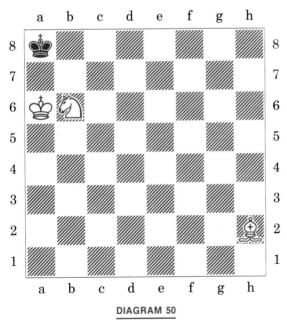

DIAGRAM 50

Checkmate by knight and bishop.

What is Stalemate?

If one side simply runs out of legal moves, and it is not checkmate, then the game ends in a draw by stalemate. This is most likely to occur in the endgame, when one side only has a king left. Stalemate often arises when one player has a huge material advantage, while the other has a lone king. If the player with the advantage becomes careless, stalemate is sometimes accidentally permitted. So, watch out when you are winning! Beware of stalemates!!

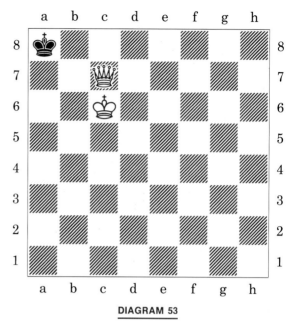

DIAGRAM 53

Black to play has no moves that are legal. Also a draw by stalemate.

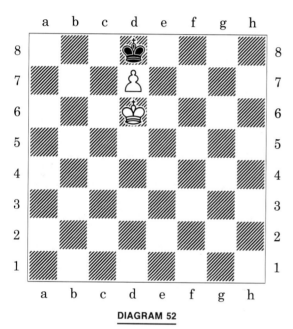

DIAGRAM 52

Black to play has no moves, therefore, a draw by stalemate.

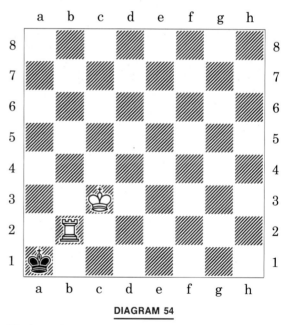

DIAGRAM 54

Black to play again has no legal move. Stalemate!

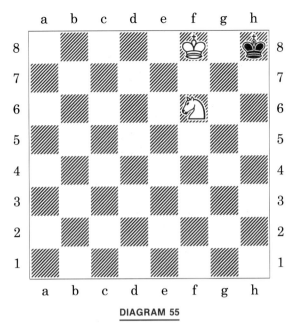

DIAGRAM 55

Another stalemate, with Black to play, this time with the knight.

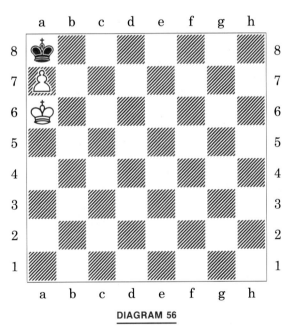

DIAGRAM 56

Black to move — stalemate! If Black can get his king to the promotion square, a lone defending king can always draw against king and a-pawn or king and h-pawn.

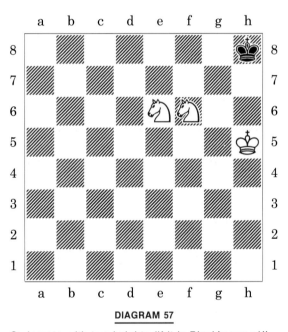

DIAGRAM 57

Stalemate with two knights (if it is Black's move)!!

How Draws Come About

Apart from stalemate and agreement, there are other ways to draw. If exactly the same position occurs three times in a game, with the same side to move, then the game is drawn. This is a draw by threefold repetition of position.

A similar case is perpetual check, where a series of checks to one player's king also leads to the same position occurring three times.

Finally, you should note which positions are drawn due to insufficient material to give checkmate. Some endgame positions can be drawn, even if a player is heavily down on material. For example:

king against king is obviously a draw;

king and bishop against a lone king is always a draw;

king and knight against a lone king is always a draw;

king and two knights against a lone king is also, amazingly, a draw, but only if the weaker side defends correctly — there are possible checkmates in this endgame;

king and pawn against a lone king is sometimes drawn — it depends on the relative positions of the kings.

Do not worry about memorising the above list. If you enter an endgame of king and knight or king and bishop against a lone king it is physically unwinnable, so you do not need to know any special manoeuvres. Also, the ending of king and two knights vs lone king is so rare that it is hardly worth bothering with. However, since it is very common, you must know when the endgame of king and pawn vs lone king is a win and when it is a draw. This endgame is so important that it is dealt with in detail under the heading KING AND PAWN AGAINST KING.

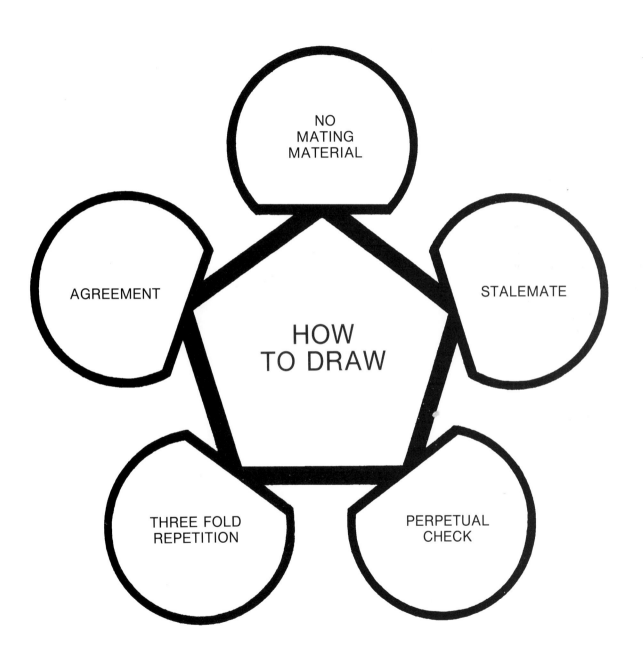

Scholar's Mate

The sequence of moves **1 e2–e4 e7–e5 2 ♗f1–c4 ♗f8–c5 3 ♕d1–h5 ♘b8–c6 4 ♕h5xf7** mate is known as Scholar's Mate. More beginners fall prey to Scholar's Mate than to any other set of winning moves. This opening trap must, therefore, be learnt!

Although this is, in fact, an elementary trap, the moves of Scholar's Mate are highly instructive. They demonstrate the use of the diagonal in chess, as White exploits the light-coloured squares in order to deliver mate. Scholar's Mate also highlights some basic precepts in chess play — always think about the threats behind an opponent's move and try to prevent your opponent from building up pressure against a weak square in your position. In this case, the weak point for Black is f7.

Let's look at the moves in greater detail:

1   e2–e4

White's pawn moves from the starting point at e2 to e4, a traditional opening move. By moving the pawn away from e2 White has unleashed the potential power of his queen, which can now invade Black's sphere of influence via the d1–h5 diagonal. White's light-squared bishop can also mobilise to the excellent square c4 via the f1–a6 diagonal. Together these two routes will furnish deadly pressure against the vulnerable f7-square.

1   ...   e7–e5

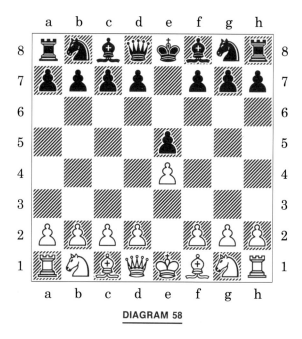

DIAGRAM 58

A sensible reply for Black, mirroring his adversary's opening bid.

2   ♗f1–c4

White's king's bishop now joins the fray and is poised for attack along the c4–f7 diagonal.

2   ...   ♗f8–c5

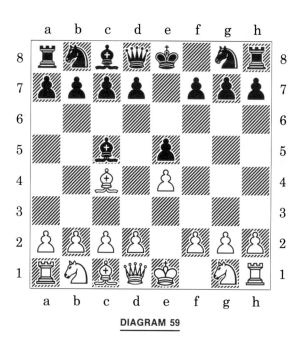

DIAGRAM 59

Black develops his bishop, again imitating the moves of his opponent.

3   ♕d1–h5

Attacking the black e-pawn, which is undefended, but also, and more worryingly for Black, adding pressure against the f7-square. The black pawn on f7 is terribly weak, because it is protected only by its own king. The white queen is now operating with huge strength along the h5–f7 diagonal.

3   ...   ♘b8–c6

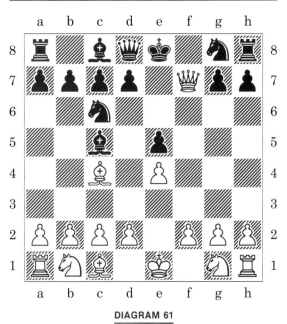

DIAGRAM 61

In this drastic example, Black contravened some simple rules of basic chess strategy by failing to spot White's threats and also failing to secure the safety of his king. In contrast, White successfully orchestrated the moves of two of his pieces to deliver a quick and efficient mate. The tactic of pushing against a weak spot, such as that provided by f7 in this example, recurs frequently in chess games and is particularly useful in staging a kingside attack.

Scholar's Mate may appear after a number of variations in Black's moves, for example 1 e2–e4 e7–e5 2 ♕d1–h5 ♘b8–c6 3 ♗f1–c4 ♘g8–f6 4 ♕h5xf7 mate. White's moves are always constant and result in a four move mate delivered on f7 by the queen which is supported by the white king's bishop from c4.

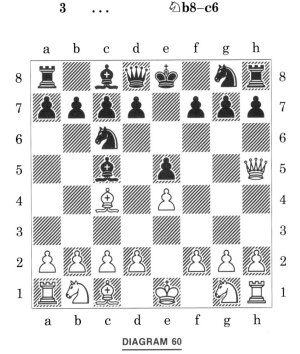

DIAGRAM 60

Protecting the e5-pawn, but ignoring the main threat. Together the white queen and bishop are ready to strike against f7. Black should play 3 ... ♕d8–e7 to stop the mate and defend the e5-pawn.

4   ♕h5xf7   MATE!

White delivers the final coup. Black's king is unable to flee and Black cannot bring any of his own pieces into play to save his monarch.

However, the reader is not recommended to play for Scholar's Mate in his or her own games. If your opponent is familiar with it then Scholar's Mate will easily be prevented and you will soon find that your queen is being chased all over the board as your opponent develops pieces with gain of time.

PUZZLES

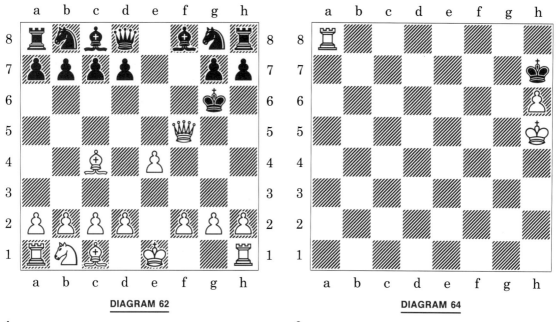

DIAGRAM 62

1

Is this checkmate?

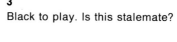

DIAGRAM 64

3

Black to play. Is this stalemate?

DIAGRAM 63

2

Is this checkmate?

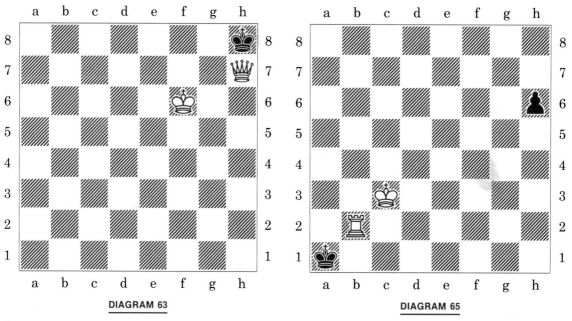

DIAGRAM 65

4

Black to play. Is this stalemate?

ANSWERS

Here again, you should score 100% if you have fully understood the material so far. If not, why not run through the material on special rules again?

1

No, this is not checkmate. Black is in check and must immediately get out of it, but he can do this by playing ... ♚g6–h6.

2

This is also not checkmate. Black can get out of the check by playing ... ♚h8xh7, since White's queen is not protected.

3

With Black to play this is a draw by stalemate since Black's king (his only piece) has no legal move.

4

No, this is not stalemate, since Black still has a legal move with his pawn, namely, ... h6–h5.

Golden Rules

These are the principles you should remember and follow when trying to win — ALWAYS! They are set out clearly to help you to commit them to memory.

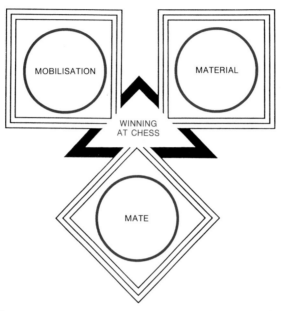

GOLDEN RULES OF MOBILISATION

Golden Rules of Material

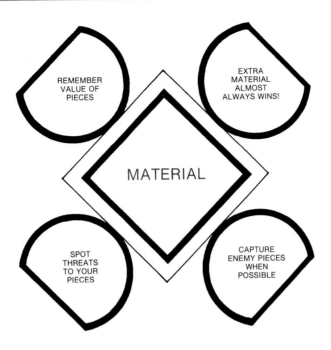

Golden Rules of Checkmate

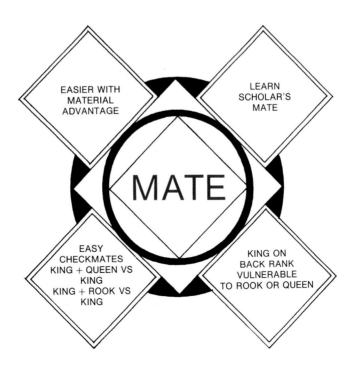

The Basic Openings

The following four opening sequences are all good and extremely reliable for both sides. You should endeavour to memorise them and use them in your games.

Giuoco Piano

Each player mobilises swiftly and efficiently in this opening.

> **1   e2–e4   e7–e5**

Both sides stake a claim in the centre and prepare to develop their king's bishops at an early stage.

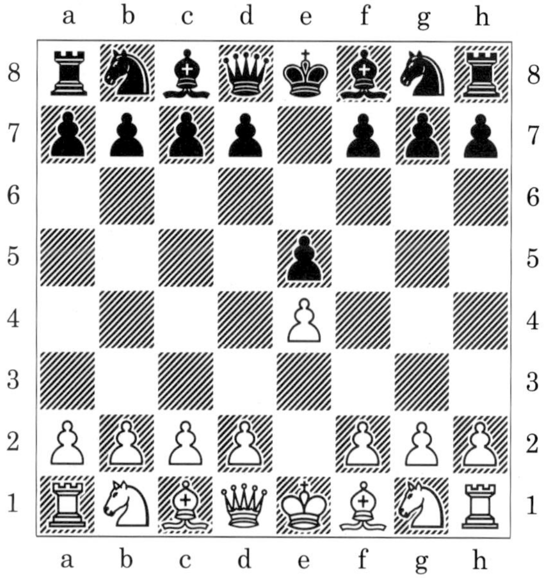

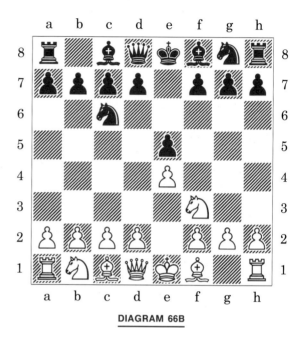

with this knight. In reply Black defends the e-pawn with his queen's knight. Both knights are well placed in the centre.

DIAGRAM 66B

> **3   ♗f1–c4   ♗f8–c5**

Both players develop their king's bishops to active squares.

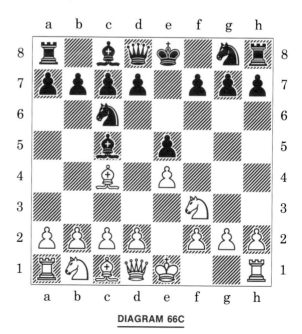

DIAGRAM 66C

DIAGRAM 66A

> **2   ♘g1–f3   ♘b8–c6**

On his second move White brings out his king's knight, attacking the black e-pawn

4   ♘b1–c3   ♞g8–f6

The other knights are brought into play. Now a perfectly symmetrical position has arisen – both sides are ready to castle and will soon try to bring their queen's bishops into play.

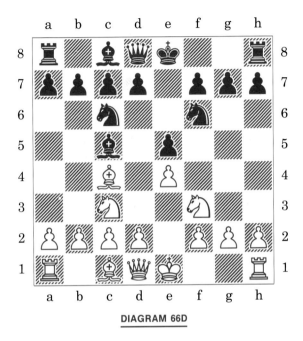

DIAGRAM 66D

Sicilian Defence

A sharp, counterattacking defence, favoured by Kasparov and Fischer.

1   e2–e4   c7–c5

Instead of replying to White's e2–e4 with ... e7–e5, Black immediately brings an unbalanced nature to the position.

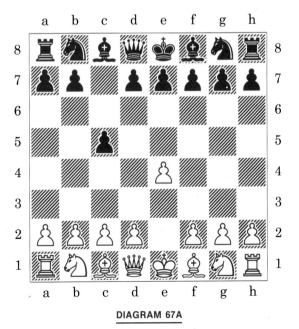

DIAGRAM 67A

2	♘g1–f3	d7–d6

White again brings his king's knight into play and Black bolsters his central position with his queen's pawn.

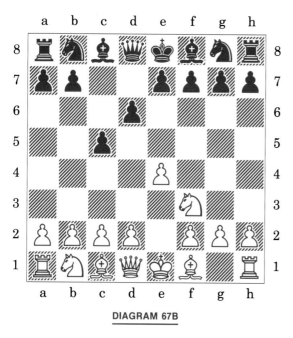

DIAGRAM 67B

3	d2–d4	c5xd4

White advances his queen's pawn in the centre and Black captures this pawn.

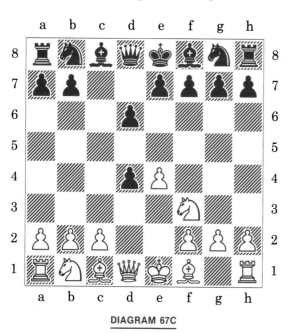

DIAGRAM 67C

4	♘f3xd4	♘g8–f6

White recaptures with his knight and Black brings out his king's knight, hitting the white e-pawn. After White defends this pawn, most likely with 5 ♘b1–c3, we arrive at an extremely rich position in which both sides have several options for future play.

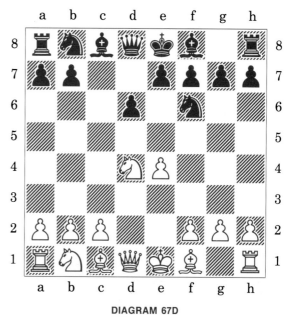

DIAGRAM 67D

declines the gambit by bolstering his d-pawn with the e-pawn.

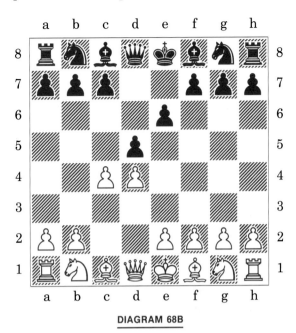

DIAGRAM 68B

Queen's Gambit Declined

Again, speedy mobilisation is a feature of this opening. It is a solid favourite of Karpov (World Champion 1975–1985).

1   d2–d4   d7–d5

This time both sides advance their queen's pawns first, each of which has important influence over the central squares.

3   ♘b1–c3   ♘g8–f6

White develops his queen's knight, putting pressure on Black's d-pawn, and Black develops his king's knight to an active square.

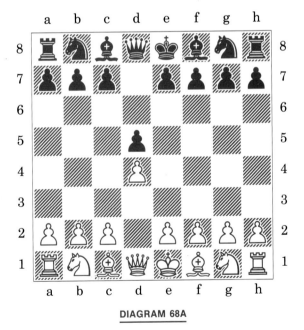

DIAGRAM 68A

2   c2–c4   e7–e6

White pushes forward his c-pawn offering a gambit which, if accepted, would offer him good chances in the centre. Black

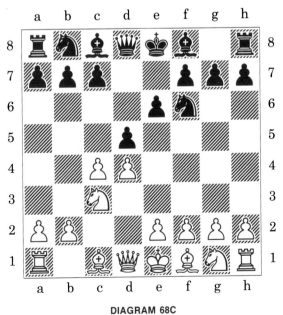

DIAGRAM 68C

4   ♗c1–g5   ♝f8–e7

White brings his queen's bishop into play, pinning the black knight to the queen, which Black meets by bringing his king's bishop out. Now Black is ready to castle and can then develop his other pieces. White has slightly more space on the board but Black's position is very solid.

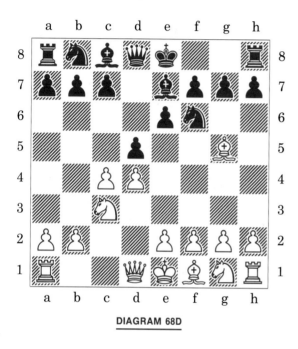

DIAGRAM 68D

English Opening

Introduced by English masters in the 1840s, this opening promises a bright future for White's active king's bishop.

1   c2–c4   e7–e5

Here White first moves his queen's bishop's pawn and Black responds by moving his king's pawn into the centre. Notice the similarity to the Sicilian Defence, except that colours are reversed!

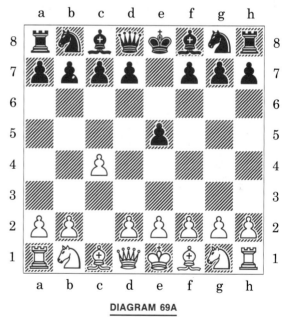

DIAGRAM 69A

2   ♘b1–c3   ♞g8–f6

Both sides bring their knights into play on central squares.

DIAGRAM 69B

3   g2–g3   ♞b8–c6

White moves forward his g-pawn, planning a 'fianchetto', whereby a bishop moves on to a 'long diagonal'. Black responds by bringing his other knight into play.

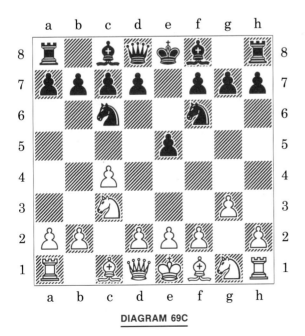

DIAGRAM 69C

4   ♗f1–g2   ♗f8–b4

White completes his fianchetto and Black swings his bishop down to b4. Black is now ready to castle and may later exchange his king's bishop for the white knight on c3.

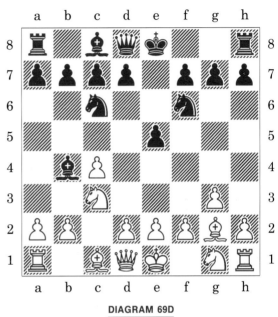

DIAGRAM 69D

The Basic Endgames

KING AND QUEEN VS KING

You must learn the basic mating positions of king and queen against lone king. They are very common and may occur frequently in your own games. The first and golden rule is that in order to give checkmate in this type of endgame you must drive the enemy king to one of the four sides of the board. If you fail to do this in such endgames, you will not be able to give checkmate.

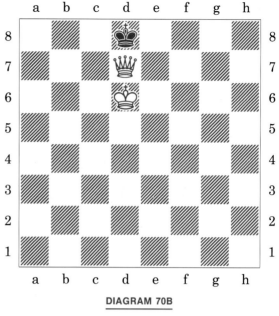

DIAGRAM 70B

Also a standard checkmate with king and queen against king.

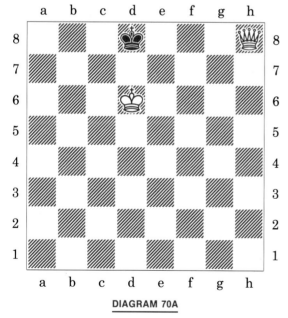

DIAGRAM 70A

This is a standard checkmating position.

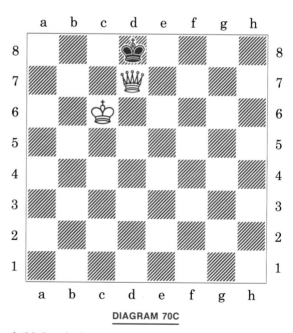

DIAGRAM 70C

A third typical mate with king and queen against king.

The mating process with king and queen against king — a typical case:

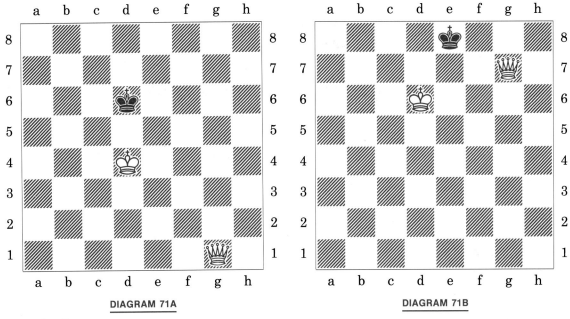

DIAGRAM 71A

DIAGRAM 71B

From the diagram:

1	♕g1–g6+	♚d6–d7
2	♔d4–d5	♚d7–e7
3	♕g6–g7+	♚e7–e8
4	♔d5–d6	

Checkmate will now come on the next move, thus

4	...	♚e8–d8
5	♕g7–d7	Mate

Notice how White had to use both his king and queen to drive Black to the edge of the board.

KING AND ROOK VS ROOK

You must also memorise the typical mating positions with king and rook against a lone king.

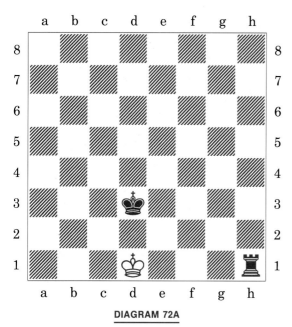

DIAGRAM 72A

This is checkmate. You must always drive the enemy king to one of the four sides of the board, otherwise it will escape.

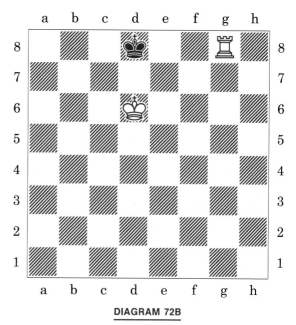

DIAGRAM 72B

This is checkmate.

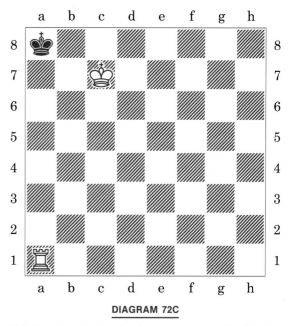

DIAGRAM 72C

This is also checkmate. As you can see, the black king has been mated along the a-file. In this endgame, the lone king must always be chased to one of the four sides of the board, either the a-file, the h-file, the first rank or the eighth rank. It is the only way to win.

Here is the winning process with king and rook against king in action:

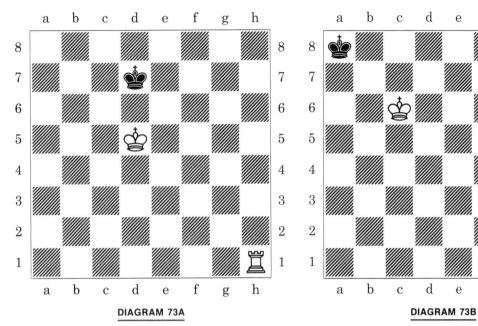

DIAGRAM 73A

DIAGRAM 73B

From the diagram, watch this procedure:

1	♖h1–h7+	♚d7–c8
2	♚d5–d6	♚c8–b8
3	♚d6–c6	♚b8–a8

4	♚c6–b6	♚a8–b8
5	♖h7–h8	Mate

This process is very easy to learn.

KING AND PAWN VS KING

This is one of the most important endgames. It occurs very frequently and it will be of great benefit to you to know which positions are draws and which positions can be won.

In some cases, the lone king will be so far away from the pawn that the pawn will simply romp home and become a queen. That is an easy win, of course. What, though, if the lone king can block the path of your extra pawn? You might think that your king could shepherd the pawn home to become a queen in all cases. Sometimes this is true, but not always. It is around 50–50 in fact, between a win and a draw.

Let's look at a typical example. This is very important and it will help you to remember the principle. If you do, you may pick up a lot of extra points in endgames.

In **Diagram 74A**, it is White's move. White can win, but the question is, how? The obvious way is to advance the passed pawn and try to make a queen. However, this is too brutal and it does not work. Let us see why.

1	d5–d6	♚d8–c8
2	d6–d7+	♚c8–d8
3	♔c6–d6	

And, as we can see from **Diagram 74B**, it is a draw by stalemate.

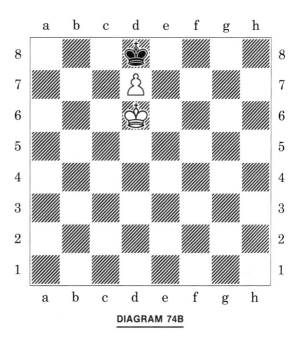

DIAGRAM 74B

DIAGRAM 74A

Let us go back to **Diagram 74A**. The way to win is, essentially, to place your king directly in front of your opponent's king. By so doing, you force it to give way. In chess parlance this is termed 'gaining the opposition'. This is the most vital principle in endgames of kings and pawns. You must remember it. It is useful not only for the attacking side, but also for the defender. Now that we know about the principle of 'gaining the opposition', see how easy it is to win from the diagram position.

1	♔c6–d6	♚d8–e8
2	♔d6–c7	♚e8–e7
3	d5–d6+	

And it is obvious that Black cannot prevent the pawn from queening.

There is one alternative variation, but it is equally simple:

1	♔c6–d6	♚d8–c8
2	♔d6–e7	♚c8–c7
3	d5–d6+	

And again, it is absolutely clear that the pawn will inevitably queen.

Zugzwang

I would like to explain zugzwang. Gaining the opposition is a very common form of 'zugzwang', a german word meaning compulsion to move. A zugzwang position is one in which the player to move will worsen his situation no matter what he does — in fact, he would prefer not to have to move at all! However, in chess you cannot pass on your move so zugzwang can be very powerful, especially in king and pawn endings such as the one we have just discussed. There Black is forced, after 1 ♔c6–d6, to play either ... ♚d8–e8 or ... ♚d8–c8, both of which allow White to advance his king.

PUZZLES

DIAGRAM 75

1
Can Black win?

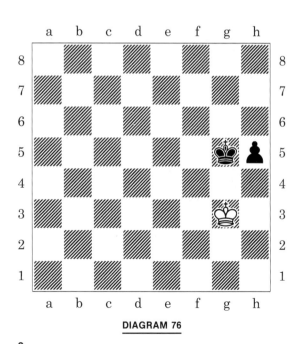

DIAGRAM 76

2
Can Black win?

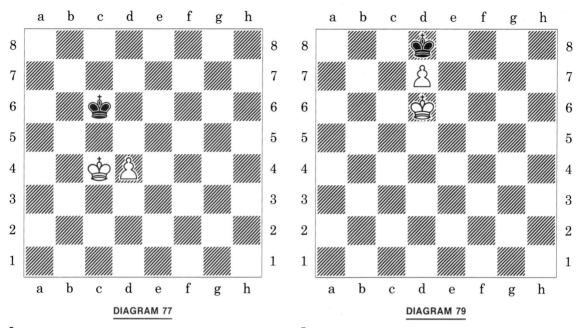

DIAGRAM 77

3

Black to move. Can White win?

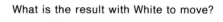

DIAGRAM 79

5

What is the result with White to move?

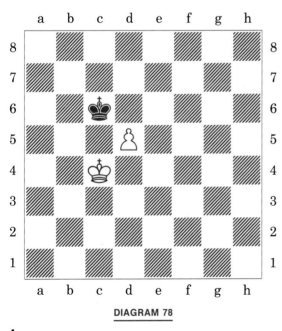

DIAGRAM 78

4

Black to move. Can White win?

ANSWERS

1

Black cannot force a win since White's king is in contact with the promotion square, a1. The side with the extra pawn can never promote it if it is on either the a- or h-file and the enemy king can reach the promotion square.

2

Black also fails to win by force in this position. The best he can achieve is draw by stalemate, e.g. 1 ♔g3–h2 ♔g5–g4 2 ♔h2–g2 h5–h4 3 ♔g2–h1 ♔g4–g3 4 ♔h1–g1 h4–h3 5 ♔g1–h1 h3–h2 stalemate.

3

If it is Black to move, he can gain the opposition and the game will be a draw. Thus, 1 ... ♔c6–d6 2 d4–d5 ♔d6–d7 3 ♔c4–c5 ♔d7–c7 4 d5–d6+ ♔c7–d7 5 ♔c5–d5 ♔d7–d8 6 ♔d5–c6 ♔d8–c8 7 d6–d7+ ♔c8–d8 8 ♔c6–d6 stalemate. However, even with White to move this position is still a draw.

4

This is also a draw after 1 ... ♔c6–d6 2 ♔c4–d4 ♔d6–d7 3 ♔d4–c5 ♔d7–c7 and, as in the previous example, White can make no further progress.

5

White, to move, wins easily with 1 ♔d6–c6 ♔d8–e7 2 ♔c6–c7 when Black cannot prevent the promotion of White's pawn.

These puzzles are quite difficult in comparison with much of the earlier material in this book. However, king and pawn endgames form the basis of so much chess practice, that these examples must be understood and memorised if you are going to win your winning positions.

Heroes

PAUL MORPHY –
The Greatest Chess Genius?

The American lawyer Paul Morphy (22 June 1837–10 July 1884) is often regarded as the greatest genius chess has ever seen. Morphy exploded onto the chess scene in the late 1850s but at the age of twelve he had already demonstrated his talents in his home town of New Orleans by beating the European master Johann Löwenthal. This established his fame as an outstanding prodigy and in 1857 Morphy, at the age of 20, dominated the field in the first American Chess Congress, held in New York, where he defeated the German master Louis Paulsen in the final.

There followed a triumphant tour of London and Paris in which Morphy stormed through European chess, scattering the most formidable masters like chaff before the wind. Meanwhile, he delighted spectators with his casual virtuoso play at blindfold chess, facing up to eight opponents simultaneously, without sight of the board. In a series of individual matches, Löwenthal, Harrwitz and Anderssen (the champion of London 1851) suffered dramatic defeats at Morphy's hands. The American's superiority was outstanding. Against Anderssen he lost two games, drew two, but won seven. His only disappointment was his failure to engage Howard Staunton, who was still the world's most famous player, if not the strongest. Had the official World Championship title then existed Morphy would surely have been the holder.

Morphy's exploits were exuberantly fêted in Europe and North America. In Paris a bust was unveiled, and dinners and presentations greeted his return home in 1859. Chess mania gripped America and plans for new clubs, tournaments and books were set in motion. Yet, in a curious and eerie premonition of Bobby Fischer's long withdrawal from public competition after his World Championship victory in 1972, Paul Morphy also chose to retire from serious combat. After his European tour Morphy never again played against first class opponents and confined himself to simultaneous displays or casual games with amateurs, to whom he gave heavy odds.

Sadly, Morphy's attempts to set up a legal practice failed and the American Civil War damaged the personal fortunes of his family. In later life Morphy developed paranoid delusions and refused even to talk about his former chess triumphs. He died in 1884 after suffering a stroke. As with Bobby Fischer, Morphy's vanishing act at the very height of his powers created a myth of super-human power in the public mind. He played a mere 75 competitive games in his career, but the belief persists that he may have been the greatest genius chess has ever seen.

Morphy's contribution to chess practice was indeed considerable. He was not only well versed in the theory of the day, he was also amazingly rapid and accurate in his play. His coruscating technique was ingenious and resourceful. Never blundering, he was also blessed with outstanding understanding of the endgame. The game which follows illustrates with crystal clarity the overwhelming impact that Morphy's play had on the international chess community of his age.

White: Paul Morphy
Black: The Duke of Brunswick and Count Isouard together in consultation
Played at Paris in 1858

1	e2–e4	e7–e5
2	♘g1–f3	d7–d6
3	d2–d4	♗c8–g4
4	d4xe5	♗g4xf3
5	♕d1xf3	d6xe5
6	♗f1–c4	♘g8–f6
7	♕f3–b3	♕d8–e7
8	♘b1–c3	c7–c6
9	♗c1–g5	b7–b5
10	♘c3xb5	c6xb5
11	♗c4xb5+	♘b8–d7
12	0–0–0	♖a8–d8
13	♖d1xd7	♖d8xd7
14	♖h1–d1	♕e7–e6
15	♗b5xd7+	♘f6xd7
16	♕b3–b8+	♘d7xb8
17	♖d1–d8	**Checkmate**

A wonderful game in which White's two remaining attacking pieces combine to deliver checkmate against almost an entire black array of forces.

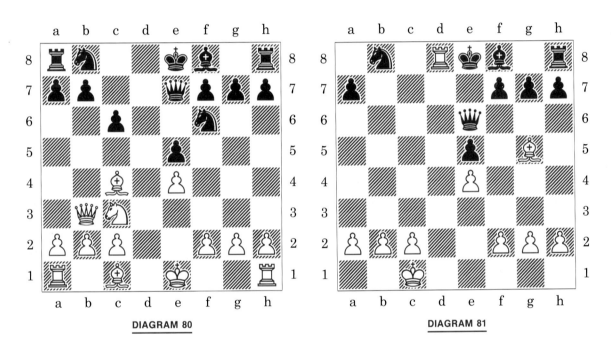

DIAGRAM 80   DIAGRAM 81

Bobby Fischer –
The Living Legend

The first American to become official World Champion was Bobby Fischer — the brash unschooled teenager from Brooklyn who toppled the might of the Soviet chess system before his 30th birthday. His story epitomised the self-reliant, frontier ideals of modern America and provided the inspiration for the Tim Rice/Abba musical CHESS. But the dream evaporated after Fischer had broken Soviet chess domination and taken the world title from Boris Spassky in 1972. Inexplicably, Fischer renounced chess totally and did not play even a single competitive game for twenty years. He did not even visit a chess club or chess event as a spectator until his return match with Boris Spassky in September 1992. Having scaled the Everest of chess achievement perhaps he had nothing more to prove to himself or to the world. His self-imposed exile recalls the seclusion of that other American genius — Paul Morphy.

Fischer's 1972 match against Spassky was characterised by the American's detailed demands and his near refusal to play before the match was even under way. Spassky had never before lost a game to his antagonist and the Russian's meticulous pre-match preparation, both mental and physical (Spassky enjoyed playing tennis to keep fit), was well known. Spassky won the first game and was awarded the second by default when Fischer failed to put in an appearance at the board.

Once Fischer had condescended to play, however, events took a miraculous course. The American began to produce magnificent chess and backed this up with a vast battery of psychological pressures, protesting about both the playing conditions and the board. He demanded the exclusive use of his hotel swimming pool and insisted that the official chess board be reduced in size by three millimetres. In retaliation the Soviet delegation alleged that Spassky was being distracted by electronic or chemical equipment and demanded a complete search of the playing hall, including an X-ray of the players' chairs which revealed merely that they contained two dead flies. The match ended with Fischer taking the title by the score of $12\frac{1}{2}$ points to $8\frac{1}{2}$.

Inevitably a clash between representatives of Russia and America became overladen with symbolic and political overtones, which attracted the glare of the world media. Perhaps the western media exposure, to which Spassky, being a Russian, was quite unaccustomed, helped to knock the stuffing out of him. After 1972 chess enthusiasts witnessed an amazing and unexpectedly permanent decline in his morale. He never again challenged for the world title.

Strangely, the 1972 match had an even more disastrous impact, in chess terms, on its victor. Fischer's self-imposed exile until 1992 angered and exasperated chess enthusiasts and the general public alike. It seemed just one more capricious exploit by the most demanding and volatile star that chess has ever known.

Yet Fischer's apparently endless demands acted as a major catalyst in improving the lot of the professional chess player. In 1969 Spassky's World Championship prize had been $1,600. In 1972 the prize fund had been boosted to an unprecedented $250,000. The prize fund for the 1993 title bout is mooted at no less than $4 million. This development came directly from Fischer's insistence that he should be renumerated on the same scale as other international celebrity sportsmen.

Fischer demonstrated, almost overnight, that chess was not just a cerebral activity for ageing intellectuals. He endowed the game with the mass appeal in the West that it had always enjoyed in the Soviet Union. Moreover, he showed that chess players could make headline news and that the game could reward individual effort and his recent return match with Spassky, for a $5 million purse, put Fischer on the front pages of the world's newspapers once again. After the 1972 match there was a massive upsurge in the popularity of chess, which continued for many years, reflecting Fischer's unprecedented contribution in bringing chess to the public eye.

White: Grandmaster Robert Byrne
Black: Bobby Fischer
Played in the US Championship at New York in 1964

1	d2–d4	♘g8–f6
2	c2–c4	g7–g6
3	g2–g3	c7–c6
4	♗f1–g2	d7–d5
5	c4xd5	c6xd5
6	♘b1–c3	♗f8–g7
7	e2–e3	0–0
8	♘g1–e2	♘b8–c6
9	0–0	b7–b6
10	b2–b3	♗c8–a6
11	♗c1–a3	♖f8–e8
12	♕d1–d2	e7–e5
13	d4xe5	♘c6xe5
14	♖f1–d1	♘e5–d3
15	♕d2–c2	♘d3xf2
16	♔g1xf2	♘f6–g4+
17	♔f2–g1	♘g4xe3
18	♕c2–d2	♘e3xg2

19	♔g1xg2	d5–d4
20	♘e2xd4	♗a6–b7+
21	♔g2–f1	♕d8–d7

Here White resigned on account of **22 ♕d2–f2 ♕d7–h3+ 23 ♔f1–g1 ♖e8–e1+ 24 ♖d1xe1 ♗g7xd4 25 ♕f2xd4 ♕h3–g2 Checkmate**

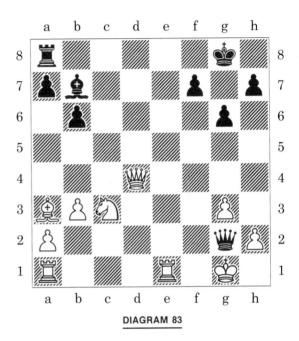

DIAGRAM 83

A stunningly beautiful and unexpected finish.

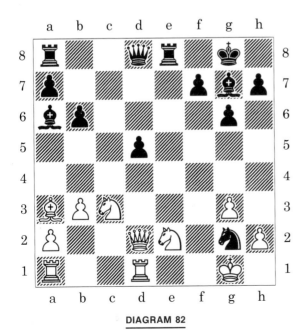

DIAGRAM 82

GARY KASPAROV –
The World Champion

Gary Kasparov ranks as the greatest player of all time. The January 1990 official FIDE (World Chess Federation) rating list gave his Elo rating as 2800, the first time a player had ever reached the magic mark and the first time that anyone had bettered Fischer's previous all time high of 2785. Kasparov was born in Baku (the capital of Azerbaijan) on April 13 1963. His chess talents shone through at an early age and he won the World Junior Championship in 1980. From then onwards, Kasparov tore through the leading ranks of grandmasters like a whirlwind. In 1982, he was equal first in the USSR Championship and thereafter took a string of clear first places in tournaments, including Brussels 1986, Reykjavik 1988 and Linares 1992. He also won major matches, to become, in 1984, the official challenger for the World Championship title. Kasparov has, since then, contested a marathon series of world title matches with his great rival, Anatoly Karpov. The second of these, in 1985, made Kasparov, aged 22, the youngest World Champion in the history of the game as an organised mental sport.

When not competing in tournaments and matches around the world, Kasparov is a tireless promoter of the intellectual and educational virtues of chess. He has given displays against entire national squads of seasoned Grandmasters and has given his services to many charitable causes. He has also been actively involved in improving conditions for professional chess players and was a prominent democrat in Russia long before the break-up of the Soviet Union.

Kasparov's playing style is that of a self-confident genius, who combines solidity and tenacious defence with fiery brilliance. He is the Napoleon of the chessboard, always blazing away with bigger and better cannons than his opponents.

Elo Ratings

Official World Chess Federation Rankings are issued twice a year. They are often known as 'Elo ratings', after the US statistician, Prof. Arpad Elo, who devised them.

Key ratings are:

Kasparov:	2805	A world record
Fischer:	2785	
Grandmaster:	2500	
Expert:	2200	

Published international ratings start at 2000, but national ratings start much lower. By playing in tournaments you can achieve a published chess rating yourself.

White: Gary Kasparov
Black: World Champion Anatoly Karpov
Played in the World Championship at Moscow in 1985

1	d2–d4	♘g8–f6
2	c2–c4	e7–e6
3	♘b1–c3	♗f8–b4
4	♘g1–f3	0–0
5	♗c1–g5	c7–c5
6	e2–e3	c5xd4
7	e3xd4	h7–h6
8	♗g5–h4	d7–d5
9	♖a1–c1	d5xc4
10	♗f1xc4	♘b8–b6
11	0–0	♗b4–e7
12	♖f1–e1	b7–b6
13	a2–a3	♗c8–b7
14	♗h4–g3	♖a8–c8

15	♗c4–a2	♗e7–d6
16	d4–d5	♘f6xd5
17	♘c3xd5	♗d6xg3
18	h2xg3	e6xd5
19	♗a2xd5	♕d8–f6
20	♕d1–a4	♖f8–d8
21	♖c1–d1	♖d8–d7
22	♕a4–g4	♖c8–d8
23	♕g4xd7	♖d8xd7
24	♖e1–e8+	♔h8–h7
25	♗d5–e4+	**Black Resigned**

On account of **25 ... g7–g6 26 ♖d1xd7 ♗b7–a6 27 ♗e4xc6 ♕f6xc6 28 ♖d7xf7 Checkmate**. The final position is a superb example of the combined power of two rooks cornering and checkmating the enemy king.

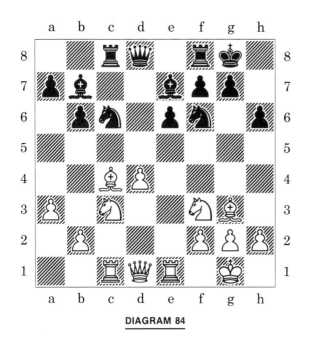

DIAGRAM 84

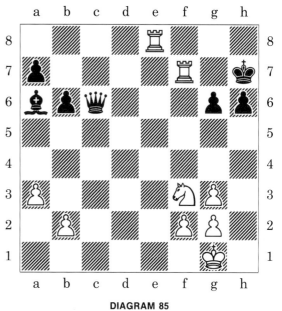

DIAGRAM 85

Nigel Short –
World Championship Challenger and Britain's Strongest Player

A twelve-year-old boy sits at a chessboard. Facing him is a formidable and deadly opponent. The man is an experienced master player, a man who has beaten one Russian World Champion and himself won the British Championship ten times. The scene is Brighton, in the summer of 1977. The boy is Nigel Short, the first pre-teenager ever to compete in the British Championship, and the hardened veteran is Dr Jonathan Penrose.

After a few moves of play, to the amazement of the onlookers, Penrose offers the boy a draw. To the even greater consternation of those looking on, the boy declines the offer. The game proceeds: first Penrose loses his queen then on the 41st move, faced with the inevitable checkmate, the shattered master concedes defeat.

That sensational game announced the arrival of a new chess prodigy, in the tradition of young geniuses of the calibre of Paul Morphy, José Capablanca and Bobby Fischer. Since his own auspicious debut, Nigel Short has progressed with meteoric brilliance. He has indisputably become the greatest British chessplayer in the history of the game. He has risen to world ranking number three and has been the inspirational leader of the grandmaster-packed English team, spearheading them to three Olympic silver medals, behind only the hitherto dominant Russians.

The culmination of Nigel Short's career so far was his victorious challenge to the living chess legend, Anatoly Karpov, in the 1992 semi-final of the World Chess Championship qualifying competition. British chess fans hope that Nigel Short will cap his brilliant career by going on to become World Chess Champion himself.

Nigel Short's Career Highlights

1977	Youngest-ever player to qualify for the British Championship where he defeats ten-times Champion Jonathan Penrose.
1979	Ties for first prize in the British Championship, missing out on the title on tie-break.
1980	Awarded the International Master (IM) title by FIDE.
1984	Becomes Britain's youngest-ever Grandmaster (GM) and wins British Championship outright.
1985	Qualifies from the Interzonal Stage to become Britain's first-ever World Championship Candidate.
1986	Defeats Gary Kasparov for the first time in an international tournament in Brussels.
1987	Qualifies for the Candidates again and regains British Championship.
1988	After beating Grandmaster Gyula Sax loses to Britain's Jon Speelman in World Championship Quarter-Final.
1990	Qualifies for the Candidates for a third time.
1991	Defeats Jon Speelman and Boris Gelfand to reach World Championship Candidates Semi-Final.
1992	Establishes new UK rating record (2685) and then upsets the odds by defeating former World Champion Anatoly Karpov in Candidates.
1993	Defeats Jan Timman for the right to challenge Gary Kasparov.

White: Grandmaster Nigel Short
Black: Grandmaster Jon Speelman
Played in the British Championship at Swansea in 1987

1	e2–e4	g7–g6
2	d2–d4	d7–d6
3	♘b1–c3	♗f8–g7
4	♗c1–e3	a7–a6
5	a2–a4	♘g8–f6
6	h2–h3	b7–b6
7	♘g1–f3	0–0
8	♗f1–c4	♘b8–c6
9	e4–e5	♘f6–e8
10	♗e3–f4	♘c6–a5
11	♗c4–a2	c7–c5
12	d4xc5	b6xc5
13	0–0	♖a8–b8
14	e5xd6	♘e8xd6
15	♘c3–d5	e7–e6
16	♗f4xd6	**Black Resigned**

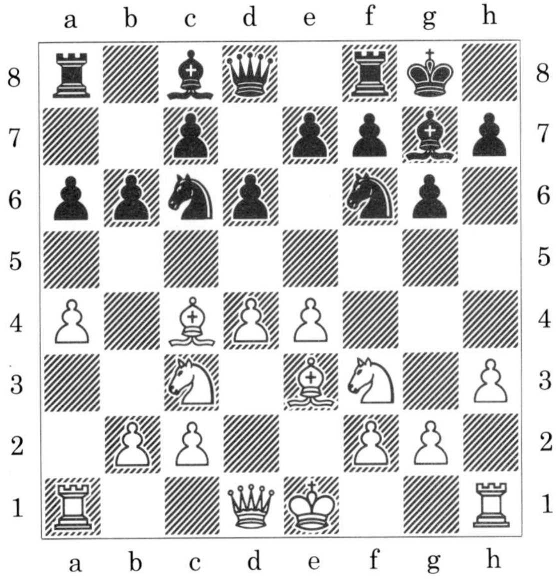

DIAGRAM 86

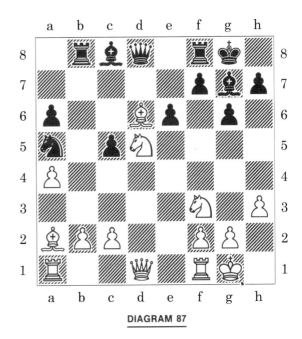

DIAGRAM 87

After **16 ... ♕d8xd6 17 ♘d5–f6+ ♗g7xf6 18 ♕d1xd6** White wins Black's queen. Or **16 ... e6xd5 17 ♗d6xb8** winning a rook. A typical and instructive case of winning on material, the most common route to victory in chess!

Chess and Computers

'Chess, the touchstone of the intellect'

GOETHE

The Past

Since the late eighteenth century, when Baron Wolfgang von Kempelen, Councillor to the Imperial Court of Vienna, constructed his chessplaying automaton, 'The Turk', there has been endless fascination with the notion of chess playing machines. Napoleon fell prey to this desire to test his own mental powers against a mechanical brain when he challenged the automaton at Schonbrunn Castle in Vienna in 1809. Of course, The Turk was not a true computer, but a mechanical device in which a human player (in this case, reputedly Allgaier, one of Vienna's strongest master players) was ingeniously concealed. Here is that historic game.

White: Napoleon Bonaparte
Black: Automaton (The Turk)
Played at Schonbrunn Castle in 1809

1	e4	e5
2	♗c4	♘c6
3	♕f3	♘f6
4	♘e2	♗c5
5	a3	d6
6	0–0	♗g4

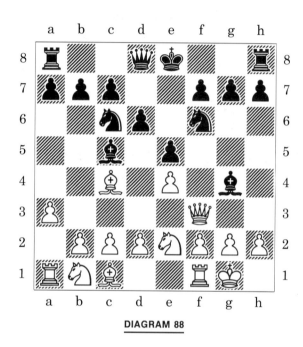

DIAGRAM 88

7	♕d3	♘h5
8	h3	♗xe2
9	♕xe2	♘f4
10	♕e1	♘d4
11	♗b3	♘xh3
12	♔h2	♕h4
13	g3	♘f3
14	♔g2	♘xe1+
15	♖xe1	♕g4
16	d3	♗xf2
17	♖h1	♕xg3
18	♔f1	♗d4
19	♔e2	♕g2
20	♔d1	♕xh1+
21	♕d2	♕g2+
22	♔e1	♘g1

23	♘c3	♗xc3+
24	bxc3	♛e2
	Checkmate	

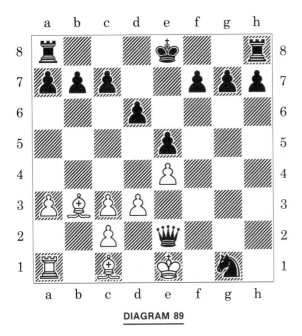

DIAGRAM 89

In many chess books, and nearly all chess columns in newspapers, an abbreviated form of chess notation is used, which does not mention the starting square of each piece. To familiarise readers with this type of notation, I give the above game in the common abbreviated form. This will stand you in good stead if you wish to follow chess games in the press.

The Present

In 1989, experts on genuine chess-playing computers were confidently predicting that within five years the best machines would be able to outplay the human World Champion. So far, thankfully, grandmasters are still warding off the challenge, in spite of the fact that IBM is enthusiastically funding the upgrading of the world's most dangerous chessplaying computer, Deep Thought. Deep Thought Mark 1 could see a staggering 750,000 chess positions per second, while Deep Thought Mark 2, with IBM's assistance, has pushed this up to ten million. In order to defeat Kasparov, their goal is the visualisation of a staggering one billion positions per second, although evidently there would be some technical difficulties in achieving this astronomical feat of calculation — even for a super-computer.

Chess and Science

Why are scientists so anxious to concentrate so much energy and so many resources on chess? A recent explanation advanced by various experts in the field is that chess is to the development of artificial intelligence what Drosophila Melanogaster (the fruit fly) is to genetic biology. It is well known that the fruit fly is an outstanding subject for empirical experiments. They need little food, you can enclose thousands of them under a glass dome and new generations grow in a couple of days. Chess is useful to scientists in a parallel way, since it is the intelligence game *par excellence*, in which complex decision situations can be studied and replicated on the computer.

On a less daunting scale, there are many excellent chess computers available in the shops for the home chess enthusiast, ranging from as little as £25.00 (or $50.00) up to several thousand. All of them can play well, teach openings and generally provide superb practice. I recommend that you purchase one if you want to improve.

SUGGESTIONS FOR FURTHER READING

Of all the mind games, chess has by far the greatest literature. There are books on opening theory, specific openings, and even monographs on single opening variations. Numerous studies of the middlegame and endgame have been published, as well as biographies of the greatest players, books on tournaments and matches and histories of chess itself.

From this vast and rich literature, my tips are:

ALEXANDER ALEKHINE — *Alekhine's Greatest Games of Chess* (Batsford)
This massive compendium of brilliant games by a great World Champion is a must for any lover of chess.

GARY KASPAROV — *Fighting Chess* (Batsford)
Kasparov's own collection of his games.

GARY KASPAROV AND RAYMOND KEENE — *Batsford Chess Openings* (Batsford)
The best source of general information on openings play. Gary Kasparov's contributions are highly original and very informative.

CATHY FORBES — *The Polgar Sisters, Training or Genius?* (Batsford)
A thrilling account of the games and training methods of the three fabulous Polgar sisters from Budapest, one of whom, Judith, may well become the first female player to win the World Championship.

RAYMOND KEENE — *Nigel Short: World Chess Challenger* (Batsford)
This is an account of the games of Britain's greatest-ever player.

DAVID LEVY AND RAYMOND KEENE — *How to Beat Your Chess Computer* (Batsford)
An easy-to-understand book on all aspects of computer chess.

TONY BUZAN — *Use Your Head* (BBC Books)
A classic book on how to improve your brain power.

Newspaper Columns and Magazines

Most major newspapers, including *The Times*, *The Guardian*, *The Daily Telegraph*, *The Independent*, *The Financial Times*, *The Observer* and *The Sunday Times*, have a regular chess column, in addition to reports on major national and international chess events.

For United States readers, there is an excellent and regular chess column written by Grandmaster Robert Byrne which appears in the *New York Times*. For international readers it should be noted that Byrne's column is also published in *The International Herald Tribune*.

Some general magazines also carry chess columns, including *The Spectator* and *New Statesman*. Many local newspapers also have a weekly column and report regularly on regional clubs and tournaments. (The columns in *The Times* and *The Spectator* are written by the author of this book.)

There are also numerous magazines that are dedicated solely to chess and which are published in Britain and abroad. One of the most famous is the *British Chess Magazine* (9 Market Street, St Leonards-on-Sea, East Sussex, TN38 0DQ, England), whilst *CHESS* magazine (369 Euston Road, London NW1 3AR, England) is also very popular, and for the US market, *Chess Life Magazine* (186 Route 9W, New Windsor, NY 12553, USA). *If you want to contact your national chess federation for information about playing in tournaments or joining a chess club, then either write to:*

**The British Chess Federation,
9a Grand Parade,
St Leonards-on-Sea,
East Sussex TN38 0DD
England**
or
**The US Chess Federation,
186 Route 9W,
New Windsor,
NY 12553
USA**

ENJOY YOUR CHESS ADVENTURES!

Raymond Keene
March 1993